RUSSIAN NONCONFORMITY

THE STORY OF "UNOFFICIAL" RELIGION IN RUSSIA

RUSSIAN NONCONFORMITY

SERGE BOLSHAKOFF,

D.Phil.

Philadelphia
THE WESTMINSTER PRESS

To the Memory of
WILLIAM TEMPLE, D.D.,
*98th Archbishop of Canterbury, Primate of All Eng-
land, Chairman of the Provisional Committee of the
World Council of Churches, Member of St. John
Damascene Society*

FOREWORD

Dr. Bolshakoff's book on Russian Nonconformity is very
timely and is most welcome. Because of the prominence of
Russia in the world of our day it is important that those outside
of Russia learn all they can of that vast country and its people.
Christianity has so long been an integral part of the life and culture of Russia that any survey of that land which leaves it out of
account is woefully imperfect. That is true even after more than
three decades of control by antireligious Communists. Christianity survives and is probably more vigorous than any other organized pre-Communist feature of Russian civilization. Yet we have
far too few books in English on Russian Christianity. That lack
is beginning to be remedied by Russian scholars who, unwelcome
to the present regime, are in exile and residents of western Europe, Britain, or America. However, almost all such books as are
now available in English or the languages of western Europe
deal, quite understandably, primarily or exclusively with what
was once the State Church. From them we might gain the impression that this is the only form of the faith in Russia, or, if
not the only form, so predominant that other kinds of Christianity can be dismissed with a few words. To many, even to those
fairly familiar with Russia, the statement of Dr. Bolshakoff will
bring almost incredulous surprise that in 1917, on the eve of the
Communist Revolution, there may have been as many as twenty-
five million Christians who did not conform to the State Church
and that today Christians in the Soviet Union outside what we
think of as the Russian Orthodox Church may total ten million.

7

Here and there we have had in English or some other western European language studies of Russian Nonconformity. Nowhere, however, do we have so comprehensive an account as that which Dr. Bolshakoff has given us.

We can especially welcome Dr. Bolshakoff's work because of some of its qualities. It is brief without being sketchy or superficial and therefore will commend itself to those who are not specialists on Russia and wish a survey that they can read without an undue expenditure of time. Yet it is based upon extensive research and sound scholarship. The impressive bibliography of materials in Russian and in western European languages and the references to them in the text are evidence of the many months of labor that have gone into the preparation of the little volume. Although a communicant of the Russian Orthodox Church, the author has had connections with some of the movements that he describes and treats them with as near an approach to objectivity as is possible in a subject so replete with ancient and recent controversy. Moreover, Dr. Bolshakoff puts the movements in their setting and in doing so makes us familiar with several of the great figures and streams of life in the Russian Orthodox Church.

His is a historical treatment. He tells us of the coming of Christianity to Russia, recounts something of its development, and makes intelligible the beginnings of the groups that are the main subject of his book and the reasons for their distinctive traits. This is all the more important for English readers because to most of them Russian Christianity and especially Russian Nonconformity is an utterly strange world. To be sure, Roman Catholicism has had marked influence and, indeed, is numbered among the nonconforming bodies. A few of the Churches described, notably the Stundists and the Baptists, owe something to Protestantism. Moreover, Russian Christianity is primarily the child of the Orthodox branch of the faith and is deeply indebted to the Greek Orthodox Church. Yet Russian Christianity bears indelibly the impress of its Russian environment and this is especially true of the movements with which the book is primarily concerned. These movements are, therefore, easily misunderstood by those who have been reared in the Western forms of Christianity, or they appear to be utterly bizarre and incomprehensible. It is one of the greatest services of Dr. Bolshakoff that the treatment he has given us enables us to see why it was that what may appear to be some of the strangest of the groups, quite alien to the Christian tradition, could be espoused by rational human beings.

The historical approach is peculiarly enlightening. Some of the movements that Dr. Bolshakoff describes have long since disappeared. Yet often they contributed to the rise of groups that are still in existence and the latter, when traced to their genesis, are much more readily comprehended than if this had not been done. Then, too, since Dr. Bolshakoff brings his story down to the present, through the insight that he has given us into the stream of history we are the better prepared to feel at home in the Russia of today. Here is a book which none who wish to understand the Russia with which we have to do can afford to ignore.

KENNETH SCOTT LATOURETTE,
Sterling Professor of Missions and
Oriental History, Yale University.

CONTENTS

INTRODUCTION

The present study of Russian Nonconformity aims to give to the English-speaking reader an adequate and documented survey of Russian Nonconformity with its struggles for religious freedom and social justice in Russia. The Nonconformists are those who refuse to conform to the State-prescribed pattern of religion, and they are by definition champions of religious freedom. It is true that many Nonconformists, once they attain power, turn out to be the worst persecutors; yet while they oppose the State they act as the champions of religious freedom. A good many Nonconformists, however, actually preach and practice religious toleration, realizing that a forced conversion is not a conversion at all.

In the present study the term "Russian" is applied to all the descendants of the Slavs of Kievan Russia: the Great Russians, commonly called the Russians and, sometimes, the Muscovites; the Ukrainians and, also, the Ruthenians and the Rusins; and the White Russians, otherwise, the White Ruthenians or the Belo-Russians. All these designations are used in the book. The term "Nonconformist" in this study includes not only those who opposed the Established Church on whatever ground and then left it but also those who, without leaving the Established or Dominant Church, formed within it an opposition to State intervention in religious affairs. The term "Church" denotes only a Christian denomination and is not applied to any other religious or political association.

In accordance with these definitions a great variety of groups or denominations, formerly called sects, are included in the survey. As it is impossible to describe all these groups without continually referring to the Russian Orthodox Church, and to Russian and Polish secular history, these backgrounds are touched upon.

In all former studies of Russian Nonconformity only the Raskolniks, who left the Russia Church in the seventeenth century, and the so-called Russian rationalist and mystical sects have been included. The Uniates, those who submitted to Rome in the sixteenth century, were never included but were treated separately in the history of the Russian Church and then merely in reference to it. The Russian Catholics rarely have been studied. The opposition to the synodal regime in Russia and divisions in the Russian Church during the Soviet Revolution and abroad are new elements previously untouched or only very slightly considered. In the pages that follow, the Raskolniks, the sects, the Uniates, and the Russian Catholics as well as the latest developments in the Russian Church are studied.

Following the introduction, the main body of this work is divided into eleven chapters. The first three study the origin of Russian Christianity, the early Novgorodian Nonconformity, and the rise of the " third Rome " idea, which effectively transformed Russian history. The next three chapters deal with the origin, development, and present state of the Raskol (the great schism) in its principal ramifications. The seventh, eighth, and ninth chapters describe Russian mystical sects, Russian native Protestants, and the Baptists. The next chapter gives an account of the Ruthenian (Ukrainian and White Russian) Uniates and the Russian Catholics, most of whom were Great Russians who adopted the Latin rite. This section also includes a description of some Russian Latinizers who never were actually Roman Catholics themselves. The last chapter describes the opposition to the synodal regime within the Russian Orthodox Church and the changes brought to the Church by the Soviet Revolution, which turned the Orthodox Church itself into a Nonconformist body. This chapter also discusses various groups that have separated from the Russian patriarchate since the Revolution. In a closing section

entitled " The Outlook," I have attempted to make some suggestions as to the probable fate and future significance of the major
living movements treated in this work.

Russian Nonconformity was not a small, insignificant movement. On the contrary, there were many millions of Nonconformists in the Russian empire.[1] In 1859 the imperial Government reluctantly admitted that the probable number of the
Nonconformists was about 9,300,000 [2] instead of the official figure
of 829,971.[3] The Statistical Committee, appointed by Count Pe-
rovsky, found that previous information was grossly inaccurate.
While officially there were but 20,240 Nonconformists in the
province of Nizhnii Novgorod, the committee discovered 172,-
600; [4] and Jeremiah, the bishop of Nizhnii Novgorod, considered
them to be as many as 233,323.[5] In Yaroslavl province 278,417
Nonconformists were found instead of the official 7,454,[6] and
I. Aksakov believed them to be 672,687 strong.

After much checking and verifying, the Government agreed
in 1863 to accept the figure of 8,220,000 as accurate. Out of this
number the Government listed 5,000,000 as Priestist Raskolniks,
2,000,000 as Shore Dwellers, 1,000,000 as Theodosians, while the
Molokans, Dukhobors, Khlysty, and Skoptsy were listed at 220,-
000 as a combined group. The latter figures were manifestly
guesswork. The sect of the Saviourites, estimated to be 700,000
strong, was altogether omitted.[7]

The Priestist prelate Yuzov considered that in 1880 the number of the Nonconformists could be estimated at 13,000,000, of
whom he listed 3,640,000 persons as Priestists, 7,150,000 as Priestless, 1,000,000 as Spiritual Christians (Molokans, Dukhobors, and
Stundists), and 65,000 as Khlysty. He added, besides, 1,145,000
persons of indeterminate faith.[8] While with the normal increase
of population the number of Nonconformists should have reached
20,000,000 by 1900, the Russian Government estimated them at
2,135,738 in 1897. Palmieri, a student of the Russian synodal
Church, thought their number to be near 15,000,000. According
to P. Miliukov the number of the Nonconformists by 1917 must
have been 25,000,000, of whom 6,000,000 were sectarians, that is,
non-Raskolniks.[9] The Priestist archbishop Irenarch Parfenov con-

siders the number of the Old Believers (Raskolniks) in 1917 to
have been about 20,000,000. All these figures represent a considerable amount of guesswork.

How many of these Nonconformists survived the Soviet Revolution it is difficult to say. The Priestist Old Believers, according
to Irenarch Parfenov, number now 3,000,000 faithful. The All
Soviet Union of the Baptists and the Evangelical Christians
claimed in 1942 to speak for 4,000,000 believers. This gives 7,000,-
000 to the Russian Nonconformists according to their own declarations. It seems probable, however, that their number is larger.
Several Priestless communities survived; but since they have no
central authority and no regular ministry, their number is entirely unknown. Again the Pentecostals were not included in the
declaration of the Baptist-Evangelical Union, which they joined
later. It is possible, therefore, that as many as 10,000,000 Russian
Nonconformists still survive in the Soviet Union.

The Uniates also run into several millions. According to Cardinal Tisserant, information from the latest available statistics of
the Ruthenian Catholics, that is, the Ukrainian and White Russian Uniates, shows them to be 5,682,819 persons strong. Nearly
all of them live either in the newly annexed territories of the Soviet Union or abroad. In Russia itself, as well as abroad, there
are millions of Orthodox descendants of several millions of the
Uniates, who joined the Orthodox Church in the eighteenth and
the nineteenth centuries.

So much for numbers. The importance of Russian Nonconformity is not to be estimated in terms of statistics. It has not
been widely realized that Russian Nonconformity in its broadest
meaning not only deeply influenced the history of Russia but
also that of many other lands. Leo Tolstoy had a few disciples in
Russia, but his teaching greatly impressed Gandhi and produced
very great results indeed. That strange Orthodox mystic, Nilus,
publisher of the protocols of Elders of Sion and other books, confirmed Adolf Hitler in his anti-Jewish and racialist views, and
thus hastened the Second World War. Bakunin's violent atheism
dominated the Bolsheviks for years and is not yet given up altogether. How far Bakunin and Herzen influenced the Bolshevik

leaders, particularly Lenin, may only be guessed. All these men were Orthodox before they rebelled against the Church and Christianity, not wishing to conform to the official Orthodoxy of their age. Some of them, like Nilus, in spite of their obviously unchristian views, died Orthodox. Again, Helen Blavatsky, hardly known in Russia, founded the Theosophist movement and revived in the West a lively interest in Eastern religions.

While not all the persons referred to above could be called Christian, the Russian Nonconformists produced many fine religious leaders and thinkers who contributed to the development of religious thought in Russia and elsewhere. Many of these people were Russian Catholics. Vladimir Soloviev greatly influenced Russian religious thought; and Bulgakov, Berdyaev, Florensky, and even Dostoevsky, were in one way or another impressed by him. The great Ukrainian Uniate leader Metropolitan Andrew Sheptitsky, the French Jesuit Bishop d'Herbigny, and others outside Russia came under his spell. Another great Russian Nonconformist was Prince Dimitri Golitsyn, Apostle of the Alleghenies, who was the first Roman Catholic priest to be ordained in the United States. Madame Svechin contributed a very great deal indeed to the revival of French Catholicism after the Great Revolution, and the Jesuits themselves are deeply indebted for their survival to Catherine II and Paul I of Russia.

The Russian Protestants, like Pavlov and Prokhanov, although never attaining the international influence of the Russian Catholics, produced a mighty religious movement within Russia and inspired the Baptists elsewhere. Some of the great Russian Nonconformists such as Archpriest Avvakum and Gregory Skovoroda only recently have begun to attract the attention of the students abroad; but their influence has been wide and profound in Russia itself for many years.

Russian Nonconformity, broadly speaking, was a protest against State intervention in the affairs of the Church. This was very largely so in the case of the Raskol in Muscovy and of the Cossack wars in the Ukraine. The Raskolniks protested against Nikon's reforms imposed by the State on the faithful against their wishes, while the Cossacks objected to the forcible introduction of the union with Rome in the Ukraine. Similarly the Russian New Nonconformists (those who today oppose the patriarchate of Moscow) justify their policy by claiming that the Russian patriarchate is not free but merely a tool of State intervention in the affairs of the Church.

Russian Nonconformity, however, is not merely a protest against State intervention in the affairs of the Church; it is also a protest against the secularization of the Church and the clerical support of social injustice. The earliest Russian Nonconformists, the Strigolniks, left the Church because they believed that it had become too worldly and had betrayed its mission. The Russian mystical sects in later times always reproached the Church for its worldliness and so did many of the Priestless. In Russian history Nonconformity nearly always stood on the side of democratic ideals and in favor of a free Church in a free State.

In a sense Nonconformity may be thought of as a natural expression of Slavonic elements in Russian life. Russian Nonconformity was born in the great northern republics of Novgorod and Pskov, whose ruling classes contained strong Slavonic elements. It flourished in Russia among free Slavonic peasants of the north and in Siberia, among the Cossacks, and among the adventurous merchants of Moscow and of the Volga. Nonconformity has seemed well suited to the Slavs. Although it is foolish and profitless to generalize about nations and races, it could be said, nevertheless, that the Slavs have been a democratic and freedom-loving people inclined to factions and anarchy. Perhaps because of this Slavonic propensity, none of the Slavic peoples has been able to create a great, strong, and lasting empire — except the Muscovites.

Many reasons have been advanced to explain the rise of the Muscovite state, which was the focal point against which most of the Nonconformists resisted. Some of the explanations are: the greater mixture of non-Slav blood, Scandinavian or Finnish; the autocratic temper of the Suzdal princes, ancestors of the czars of Muscovy; the influence of Mongol administration on the court of the princes of Moscow. Yet, neither the Finns nor the Scandinavians, nor even the Mongols, were able to create a lasting empire. And although there are many similarities between the organization of the Muscovite administration and that of the Mongols as reflected in their law, it is impossible to prove that any of the princes of Moscow were aware of these similarities. Finally, the Suzdal princes never were such autocrats as some have thought.

The best and easiest explanation of the rise of Moscow lies in its adoption of the Roman imperial idea via Byzantium. This idea of the world-wide centralized and bureaucratic state presided over by a semidivine ruler, the supreme guardian of its philosophy of life, was first planted in Russia in the reign of Ivan III, husband of Sophia Palaeologos, in the fifteenth century. In the reign of their son, Basil III, this idea was formulated by Abbot Philotheus in his concept of Moscow as the third Rome. The Muscovite sovereign was held to be the only Christian ruler in the world, the protector of Orthodoxy. The first two Romes fell on account of their falling away from Orthodoxy. Moscow is the third and the last Rome, fated to dominate the world until the end of time. Obedience to the sovereign, is, therefore, the supreme duty for everyone, cleric or layman.

Ivan IV, the Terrible, son of Basil, became in the sixteenth century the first crowned czar of Russia; and in the reign of his son, Theodore, who established the Russian patriarchate, the Byzantine system was finally adopted. As it must have been expected, the Slavonic element in Russia rebelled against these innovations. The northern republics, Novgorod and Pskov, tried to resist but were defeated and suppressed. The great Russian nobles, descendants of the princes of the house of Rurik, who considered the Muscovite sovereign merely a *primus inter pares* obliged to consult them and to rule with them, resisted for a time but were equally reduced. The crown created its own gentry, a new bureaucracy to dominate the empire as in Byzantium.

The Russian churchmen did not take too kindly their subservience to the State under a new dispensation. The new regime reduced the powerful Russian primate, who had dominated the Russian stage for centuries and was an arbiter among the feudal princes, to the position of a court prelate appointed and removed by the sovereign at will and obliged to assist the sovereign in his various and often distasteful enterprises. The Russian Church was for a long time very successful in its resistance to the idea of *rex sacerdos,* but after the defeat of Patriarch Nikon and the establishment of the Holy Synod in 1721, it too was subdued although not altogether subjugated.

The Slavonic popular masses resisted for a very long time the new scheme of the Government with its serfdom, suppression of democratic institutions, and centralized bureaucracy. Nevertheless, neither the Time of Troubles nor the gigantic rebellion of Razin and Pugachev succeeded in their aim to establish in Russia a popular, highly democratic, Cossack regime. In time, all Slavonic democratic institutions disappeared, and only the village community survived.

The same Byzantine organization enabled Moscow to absorb peacefully or to defeat and to conquer one after another the neighboring Slavonic states: Novgorod, Pskov, Ryazan, the Don Cossacks, the Ukraine, and Poland. These states with their free institutions, party strife, conflicting interests, and the absence of a single guiding idea were no match for Moscow. The Slavonic states were not alone to fall before Moscow. Soon afterward the Moslem states in the east and in the south suffered the same fate: Kazan and Astrakhan, Siberia and Crimea were absorbed, while Turkey and Persia were reduced to third rank among the powers. In the west, Sweden was reduced. Finally, at present, the Soviet Union, successor to the Russian ideas of Abbot Philotheus, Nikon, Khomiakov, Dostoevsky, Herzen, and Soloviev, dominates much of Europe and Asia.

The "third Rome" ideology was Westernized by Peter the Great and made Marxism by Lenin and Stalin. Instead of being the single Orthodox state in the world with a mission to convert its population to Christ, Russia was declared to be the single Communist state in the world with a mission to convert it to Marxism. Messianism remained and so did the imperial bureaucracy, suitably reclothed. The proselytizing as well as the striking power of the Soviet state is incomparably greater than that of the empire. But it is precisely against this background of Moscow as the third Rome with Marxism as its official religion that Russian Nonconformity is significant in this day. The story of Nonconformity told in the following pages reveals how impossible it has been to suppress freedom of religious expression in Russia. Nonconformist groups, even when persecuted and destroyed officially, have survived and have continued their influence. The story of Nonconformity, therefore, provides one of the most encouraging bases of hope for the future of Christianity in Russia.

The present study is an elaboration of a course of lectures delivered at Christ Church College at the University of Oxford, of which I am a member, in 1945 and 1946. When preparing these lectures I asked my late friend, Dr. William Temple, Archbishop of Canterbury and Chairman of the Provisional Committee of the World Council of Churches, to allow me to dedicate to him these lectures when published as a humble tribute to his kindness to me. Indeed, he prefaced my book *The Doctrine of the Unity of the Church in the Works of Khomyakov and Moehler,* which was published in 1946. The late archbishop agreed. This is not the place to dwell on my relations with this astonishing man, the greatest Englishman I have ever met and one of the greatest Christians of our age. I hope to publish at a later time the story of my relations with him, our talks and correspondence.

I must also pay a tribute to the late Dr. J. H. Rushbrooke, President of the World Baptist Alliance, who read the chapters of my study devoted to the Raskol and Russian Protestantism and who gave me some sound advice. The chapter on the Baptists was largely rewritten on his advice and to him I dedicate it.

I also thank His Eminence, Cardinal Eugène Tisserant, Bishop of Porto and Santa Rufina, Secretary to the Sacred Congregation for the Eastern Church in Rome, who communicated to me the latest statistics on the Ruthenian Catholics and was interested in my efforts to give the history of Russian Catholicism in connection with the story of Russian Nonconformity.

Finally, I express my gratitude to Professor K. S. Latourette, of Yale University, who kindly agreed to preface this study; to the directors of The Westminster Press, Philadelphia, who undertook to publish this book, particularly to Dr. Paul L. Meacham, who supervised the publication; and to the Superior General and the Fathers of the Society of St. John the Evangelist in Oxford, whose unfailing generosity helped me so much during the time when this study was elaborated.

SERGE BOLSHAKOFF.

Oxford, Michaelmas, 1949

I.

THE RUSSIAN MEDIEVAL CHURCH

The Russian Slavs who inhabited eastern Europe in the early Middle Ages were nature worshipers. They lived in small, scattered communities and occupied themselves with hunting and agriculture. Economically these little communities had a certain organization, but politically they had neither cohesion nor unity. The Scandinavian adventurers and traders who traveled from the Baltic to the Black Sea along the Russian rivers in order to trade with the Byzantine Empire or to rob its provinces, however, gradually subjected to their dominion the Slavonic tribes who lived around them. In the ninth century the Normans united most of the Slavonic tribes of European Russia into one loosely organized state with its capital at Kiev.

Christianity became the religion of Russia in 988 when Vladimir, great prince or grand duke of Kiev and great-grandson of Rurik, founder of the Russian state, persuaded the population of his capital to be baptized.[1] Vladimir, who was an able statesman, realized that his enormous but poorly organized state, based as it was on an uneasy alliance of Scandinavian adventurers, Slavonic traders and peasants, and Finnish hunters, could not survive for long unless it was unified by a common religion and culture. These unifying elements Vladimir obtained from the Byzantine Empire; but how he did it, whether directly or through Bulgaria, we really do not know. Nevertheless we do know that the Russian Church very soon became an ecclesiastical province of the patriarchate of Constantinople, taking from it doctrine, rites, customs, and manners. For more than two centuries the overwhelming majority of the Russian primates and a good many bishops were Byzantine in origin.[2]

In Russia Christianity was preached not in Greek but in the Slavonic dialect of Macedonia, which hardly differed from that of the Russian Slavs. Two Byzantines, Saint Cyril and Saint Methodius, who were very active in the ninth century, composed a special alphabet for the Slavs in order that they might be evangelized. The Bible and liturgical books were soon translated into Slavonic; and the evangelization of the Slavs proceeded, thanks to them, with a greater speed than among the Germanic tribes who were forced to master Latin. Whether the use of the Slavonic language by the Russian Church was really an advantage or not it is difficult to say. On the one hand Christian teaching was absorbed by the Russian Slavs more quickly, and the Church became a national institution. On the other hand, however, the Russian clergy, delivered from the necessity of learning the Greek language, never were stimulated to study the rich Byzantine literature in the same way that the Western clergy, forced to learn the Latin, studied the Latin ecclesiastical treatises.

The introduction of Christianity to southern Russia did not meet with any serious resistance because the Slavonic tribes did not possess temples or a regular priesthood. Some resistance to Christian propaganda was organized in Novgorod, in the north, by a pagan priest Bogomil and a nobleman Ugoniai. This resistance, however, was soon overcome. It is believed that all the Slavonic tribes of Russia were baptized under Saint Vladimir, and under his successors many Finnish tribes in the north and on the Volga were baptized and often Slavicized. This fusion of Slavs and Finns produced in due course the mightiest Russian tribe — the Great Russians. Although the Russians became nominally Christian, they preserved for a long time their pagan superstitions and rites and adapted them in many ways to their new religion just as did the new Christians in all other European nations.

As in the Latin West, so in Russia the monasteries were the chief centers for the evangelization of the country. The Lavra of Grottoes (the Monastery of the Caves) in Kiev, founded in 1062, played a great part in the evangelization of Russia. Its rule, based on that of Saint Theodore the Studite, became the foundation for all subsequent monastic rules in Russia. The Lavra founded many daughter houses and its monks helped to complete the evangelization of such pagans as still remained in the Russian state.[3] The monks of the Lavra also did much for the people with their writings and translations. They produced a good many original works in the vernacular, including the lives of saints, Russian chronicles, sermons, essays, and liturgical hymns and prayers. All these works are preoccupied with the problem of eternal salvation and try to show the right way to heaven.

In the famous *Paterik,* Bishop Simon of Vladimir and monk Polycarp in the thirteenth century inculcated religious and moral maxims in the form of parables and tales, understandable to simple folk. They taught the need for a Christian humility, meekness, poverty of spirit, and simplicity of life; but they taught also that external piety without internal conversion cannot save. Saint Nestor in his lives of Saint Boris and Saint Gleb praised these martyr princes for their Christian conduct. Wronged by their brother and knowing that he wanted to murder them, they neither rebelled nor ran away but went to the grand duke when they were summoned and died victims of injustice. Yet their cause was won.

Kievan Russia, unlike the subsequent grand duchy of Muscovy, was a federation of city states similar in many respects to those of ancient Greece and medieval Italy. Each city was ruled by a popular assembly called the veche, which elected the city magistrates as well as the agents to rule the countryside. The house of Rurik unified these independent states into a loose commonwealth very much as the British crown links together the British dominions and colonies. Yaroslav the Wise, son of Saint Vladimir, apostle of Russia, who died in 1054, divided his dominions among his numerous sons in such a way that the eldest received Kiev with the grand-ducal title and the overlordship of Russia, while the rest received other principalities in which they were *de facto* independent. The grand duke and the princes were succeeded not by their sons but by their brothers first and then by the second generation. The result was that the authority of the

grand duke became a shadow, and the princes engaged in continuous struggle among themselves for better principalities. In
these struggles they depended on the support of the Russian primates and bishops on one side and on that of the popular assemblies on the other.

The Russian Church in 1015 numbered eight dioceses. The
metropolitan of Kiev headed the Russian bishops and enjoyed a
great income and moral authority, being an arbiter among the
princes. The bishops enjoyed the same authority within their
dioceses and were powerful territorial magnates. The bishops, to
their honor, did not often abuse their opportunities. In many in-
stances they were Byzantine in background and were refined, cultured, and God-fearing men, free from the bitter partisan spirit
prevalent in Russia. They cared solely for the interests of the
Church, and they furthered these interests beyond their expecta-
tions. They obtained in due course exemption from all the secular courts not only of the clergy but of the entire population of
the ecclesiastical estates, while at the same time they gained other
advantages.

On the eve of the Mongol invasion Kievan Russia was a pro-
gressive European state with fine churches, monasteries, native
literature and art, and a federation of free semidemocratic republics under the nominal rule of the house of Rurik. Unfortunately
the Kievan state lacked cohesion and unity, and this flaw hastened
the unmaking of Kievan Russia. The great Mongol army, led by
Batu Khan, grandson of Genghis Khan, invaded Russia in 1237,
and the Kievan state collapsed like a house of cards. Russian
princes, who fought separately, were overwhelmed one after another; and Vladimir, the Russian capital which succeeded Kiev,
was taken in 1238. While the Russian state collapsed in the invasion, the Church did not. The great khans of Mongolia, who
practiced religious toleration to an unbelievable extent, recognized immediately the Church's right of self-government. They
exempted the clergy from all taxation and granted freedom of
worship and religious propaganda.

The Mongols made extensive conquests in Russia, yet they
never subjected it entirely. The Western principalities, which en-

tered later into the grand duchy of Lithuania and were taken over by the Poles, remained outside of the Mongol power. Moreover, the Mongols did not turn the conquered Russia into a province ruled by Mongol governors. They simply made the Russian principalities vassal states of the great khan and the Russian grand duke supervisor over them, responsible for peace and the regular payment of tribute.[4] The Mongol invasion brought, however, great changes in Russia. Its cultural centers migrated from the south to the west (Lithuania and Poland) or to the north (Novgorod and Vladimir-Moscow). While most of the Russian principalities were devastated, Novgorod and Pskov increased in wealth and importance and manifested their independence not only in politics but in religion as well.

Nevertheless the northern republics failed to gain supremacy in Russia. Leadership passed to the small principality of Moscow which was founded in 1263 by the grand duke Saint Alexander Nevski for Prince Daniel, his youngest son. This small principality, ruled by a line of unusually gifted princes, became in 1328 the grand duchy under Ivan Kalita, Daniel's son. Ivan was a very able ruler, and he obtained from Uzbek Khan the title of grand duke, which extended his authority over all Russian principalities. Ivan also persuaded the Russian primate, Saint Peter, to reside in Moscow although the metropolitan continued to bear the title of the Metropolitan of Kiev and All Russia. The continuous support of the primates enabled the grand dukes of Moscow to accelerate the unification of Russian principalities under their dominion. In the course of time the Muscovite grand dukes united around them all principalities of central Russia, and in 1380 under Dimitri Donskoy [5] they defeated their Oriental overlords in the battle of Kulikovo. At about the same time they stopped the further encroachment of the Russian territory by the Poles and the Lithuanians, who already had subjected several western Russian principalities to their power. Thus the grand dukes of Moscow became champions of Russian independence.

The rise of the Muscovite princes changed relations between the Church and the State. Instead of a weak grand duke, barely recognized by the princes of the house of Rurik, who considered themselves his peers, there arose a powerful sovereign, who reduced these princes to the rank of simple noblemen. The primate was no longer an arbiter among numerous princes and a refined Byzantine, subject to the powerful emperor in Constantinople; rather, he became a court prelate, often a Russian subject. Indeed, the Byzantine Empire itself lost its shine. After the sack of Constantinople by the Crusaders, the rise of the Latin empire of the thirteenth century, the Lyons Union, and the growing Turkish menace, the Byzantine Empire became merely a shadow of its former self. It did not inspire awe in the Russians any more. Under these circumstances the Russian Church progressed toward independence from Constantinople, when it would have to face by itself many difficulties, internal and external, and to solve them as best it could.

The first test for the Russian Church and its ability to cope with difficult situations was provided by two powerful separatist movements that sprang up in the northern republics of Novgorod and Pskov.

II.

THE STRIGOLNIKS AND THE JUDAIZERS

The Strigolniks

Unlike the Kievan and Muscovite Russians, who blindly trusted their Byzantine masters and teachers, the Novgorodians, either because of the greater proportion of skeptical and matter-of-fact Finnish nature in them or because of the influence of Western heretics who sought asylum among them, began early to question the dogma of the Church.

The sect of the Strigolniks or "Barbers," remote ancestors of the Russian Protestants, in the fourteenth century questioned for the first time in Russia the validity of Orthodoxy. The Strigolniks' movement had its roots in the feeling among a part of the Russian clergy that it was sinful to charge a fee for ordination and other sacraments. The Tver bishop Andrew complained to the patriarch of Constantinople that the Moscow metropolitan followed this practice. The patriarch took the metropolitan's part, but Bishop Andrew was not satisfied, and sent the monk Ankindin to Constantinople to obtain personal explanation from the patriarch.

The Greek clergy actually followed the same practice as adopted by the metropolitan of Moscow, but this was done under the pretext that the fees were the reimbursement of expenses of the clergy in connection with ordination. Ankindin was told that charging fees for ordination was against the canon law, and wrote to that effect to the grand duke and "all Russian men," equating the charging of fees for ordination with simony. This epistle strengthened the trend against charging fees for ordination among Russian clergy and laity.

The founder of this sect was, it seems, a Pskov deacon named Karp, who because it was his task to barber the clergy was nicknamed the " Strigolnik." There are several other explanations of the name of the sect, but that just mentioned seems to be the most plausible. Listening frequently to the candidates for ordination complaining about the unusually high registration fees charged by the archbishop of Novgorod, Karp came to the conclusion that the bishops were ordaining clerics for money. Karp held that such ordinations involved simony and were invalid. Finally he arrived at the conclusion that orders are invalid everywhere because registration fees are universal. If sacerdotal orders are invalid, Karp taught, it becomes blasphemous to receive sacraments from the clergy.

Accordingly Karp and his followers, the Strigolniks, left the Church and formed separate communities with their own ministry recruited from pious laymen who served without remuneration. In strong contrast with the parochial clergy who were too anxious about their income and who charged high fees for their services while neglecting to teach and to preach, the Strigolnik ministers led the most edifying and humble lives. They read the Scriptures to the faithful and commented on them but refused any payment for their services. Since the Strigolniks considered the Russian ordinations invalid because simoniac and since they denied that laymen could perform the sacraments, it was only natural that they should abolish all the sacraments except that of penance. The Strigolniks also suppressed prayers for the dead, believing them to be unscriptural. The Early Christian Church was their ideal; and like most of the sectarians, they were puritans in their outlook and life. They considered ecclesiastical Christianity to be polluted and debased, its faithful and clergy pagan, and themselves to be the elect of God — true, spiritual Christians.

Although a purely Russian phenomenon, the Strigolniks have much in common with the English Lollards and other contemporary Western dissenters. The Bulgarian Bogomil, whose writings were known in Russia, might have influenced the Strigolniks although it is difficult to prove that he did. The Strigolniks appeared well before the Western Reformation, yet they were true Protestants at heart. They objected to extreme ritualism and to the neglect of the Bible, and they opposed the formalism of the clergy and its moral laxity. They protested vigorously against the wealth of the upper clergy and the monasteries, which seemed to them to be unbecoming to servants of Christ. The Strigolniks were in some respects the remote forerunners of the Russian Priestless Old Believers of the seventeenth century and of the Russian Evangelicals who crystallized finally into the modern Russian Baptists.

While the Strigolniks never were numerous, they gave much trouble to the Russian bishops; and even after Nicetas and Karp, the two deacons who were their leaders, were executed in Novgorod in 1375 the sect survived. The patriarch Nilus of Constantinople and Saint Stephen of Perm wrote against the Strigolniks, and they tried to avoid persecution by migrating from Novgorod to Pskov. Nevertheless Photius the Peloponnesian, primate of Russia, would not leave them in peace. He exhorted the Pskov authorities to suppress the sect that advised against violence or bloodshed. The Pskov Government responded by imprisoning all sectarians. After some of the older people died and others submitted to the Church, the sect, to all appearances, disappeared within a few years. In reality, however, they only " went underground." The sudden rise of the powerful sect of the Judaizers at Novgorod a few decades later can hardly be explained unless the survival of the Strigolniks is admitted.[1]

THE JUDAIZERS

The Judaizers, who became a powerful force in opposition to the Orthodox Church, owed their existence to the proselytizing propaganda of Zechariah, a Lithuanian Jew, who came to Novgorod in 1470 in the suite of Michael-Alexander Olelkovich, prince of Kiev. Zechariah (referred to in Russian sources as Skharia) converted to Judaism two Novgorodian priests, Dionysius and Alexis, who became his ardent followers. Zechariah suggested that they should fulfill the Jewish rites secretly but avoid circumcision because of the danger of being found out. For the same reason he advised both priests to continue outwardly their life as Christian clergy. After Zechariah five other learned Jews came to Novgorod in order to instruct the new converts thoroughly in the Jewish doctrine and rites. Within a few years these Jews left Russia, commissioning the two priests to propagate the Jewish creed in its mystical and cabalistic form.

Alexis and Dionysius proved to be skillful propagandists. They quickly gathered numerous converts, among whom was Gabriel, dean of St. Sophia of Novgorod. In 1479 the grand duke Ivan III, who abolished the republican constitution of Novgorod and incorporated that country into Muscovy, came to his northern capital. After meeting both leaders of the heresy, Ivan III was so impressed by their learning and apparent piety that he invited them to Moscow. Alexis, who was renamed Abraham by the Jews, became the dean of the Primatial Church of Russia; and Dionysius became a priest of the Collegiate Church of Saint Michael. The heresiarchs soon made numerous converts, including Archimandrite Zosima of Simonovsky monastery, the future Russian primate, and Theodore Kuritsyn, the chancellor of the grand duke.

For seventeen years the heresy continued to spread quietly at Novgorod and Moscow, yet none of the bishops knew about it. Not until 1487, and only then by pure chance, did Saint Gennadius, the archbishop of Novgorod, learn about the existence in his city of a secret and heretical society. Gennadius immediately reported his findings to the primate and to the grand duke. The latter instructed Gennadius to arrest the alleged heretics and to send them to Moscow. At this time Gerontius was primate of Russia (1473–1489). He was a weak prelate who had hated Gennadius and persecuted him in the past; therefore he was not disposed to persecute those whom Gennadius denounced as heretics. Gerontius not only left the heretics in peace, representing them as victims of Gennadius' injustice, but he encouraged them. He even left undisturbed reconciled heretics who again apostatized and protected at Moscow the heretics who fled from Novgorod. Only after the death of Gerontius was Gennadius able to raise the matter again. Then it was high time for something to be done, for the heretics had succeeded in raising one of themselves, Archimandrite Zosima, to the Russian primacy.

At Gennadius' request a national Church council was convened in 1490. The new primate presided at this gathering, and the lower clergy as well as the bishops and abbots were represented. Gennadius was a stern prelate and admirer of the Spanish Inquisition, the methods of which he had learned from Nicholas Poppel, the Western emperor's ambassador; and he urged the council to destroy the heretical society and to execute those who relapsed into heresy. Naturally Gennadius met strong opposition from the heretics and their friends. Ivan III disliked capital punishment; and the celebrated Russian starets of the day, Paisius Yaroslavov and Saint Nilus of Sora, opposed it in principle. So it was that the more compromised heretics succeeded in escaping with only slight punishment, and the majority remained undisturbed. Theodore Kuritsyn, chancellor and friend of Ivan III, saved his brother heretics. Instead of being uprooted, the heresy continued to spread more and more. It penetrated the court, capturing Princess Helen, daughter-in-law of Ivan III. It seemed that Muscovy would gradually give up Christianity and become Jewish, but the heretics themselves were largely responsible for the fact that this did not happen. Ivan III's wish to deprive the monasteries of a large part of their lands, in order to distribute these to his soldiers, had a great deal to do with his tolerance of the Judaizers, whose teachings had become useful to him in this respect.

The primate Zosima, thoroughly unworthy, was a drunkard and a debauchee. His behavior was so scandalous that he was deposed in 1494, and the powerful chancellor, Theodore Kuritsyn, failed in all his efforts to replace Zosima with another heretic. Simon, the new primate, was a sworn enemy of the Judaizers; but he could do nothing against them so long as the chancellor was alive. The enigmatic Theodore Kuritsyn may remind one strongly of a still more mysterious man, Gregory Rasputin, who kept the imperial family under his spell in the twentieth century. Shrewd, ingratiating Kuritsyn, like Rasputin, seemed to possess considerable psychic power, and he exercised his influence in high places.

After the death of Kuritsyn the Moscow council met in 1504 in long and stormy session. Much time was lost in the interminable discussion between those who demanded that the heretics be burned alive and those who resolutely opposed the death penalty. The more severe point of view prevailed in the end, and ruthless punishments were inflicted upon the heretics. Several of them were burned alive, and the remainder imprisoned for life. With these burnings the heresy of the Judaizers, who absorbed the earlier Strigolniks, apparently disappeared forever. Just as in the case of the Strigolniks, however, there are serious reasons for believing that the heresy of the Judaizers only " went underground " to reappear much later in the form of new and radical sects. The Moscow council of 1504 was further noteworthy because of the appearance there of the two first Russian theological schools, the Josephites and the Nonpossessors.

Russian scholars are divided in their views concerning the doctrine of the Judaizers. Some believe that they adopted simply and fully the creed of the Jews and were in fact Russian Maranos. Others suppose that the Judaizers embraced a peculiar doctrine combining freethinking Judaism and Christianity. Clearly the Judaizers denied the trinity of the Godhead and the incarnation as well as the divinity of Christ, whom they believed to be simply a man. Awaiting another messiah, the Judaizers in the meanwhile observed the law of Moses. They rejected in accordance with their main doctrine all the sacraments, the cult of saints, icons and relics, fasts, and festivals of the Church. The Judaizers limited their canon of Scripture to the Torah of Moses. For their liturgical services they used the Jewish prayer book, which was translated into Slavonic. E. Golubinsky, the greatest historian of the Russian Church, considers the Judaizers to have been nothing more or less than Jews. It is difficult to say what brand of Judaism they professed, but it seems that the Judaizers reflected Jewish mysticism and rationalism alike.[2]

The Judaizers based their heresy on the Old Testament and its arbitrary interpretation. In order to refute them on their own grounds, the Russians needed to have at hand the entire Bible in Slavonic. Although the Russians had possessed the New Testament in Slavonic from the very time of their evangelization, they still lacked several books of the Old Testament. It became imperative, therefore, to produce the entire Bible in the language of the people. Saint Gennadius, archbishop of Novgorod and chief adversary of the Judaizers, undertook the task of translation. A surprisingly broad-minded man for his age, Gennadius did not hesitate to use the Latin Vulgate and the Jewish texts for his translation, which he finished in 1493. Gennadius' Bible incorporated the older Slavonic translations from the Greek New Testament and the Septuagint. Esther was translated from the Hebrew; and several books, such as Chronicles, Ezra, Nehemiah, and Tobit, were translated from the Vulgate. Each book was provided with a preface, partly taken from the Vulgate and partly from the German Bible. Anxious for a literal translation, Gennadius frequently obscured the text and even forced an arbitrary interpretation. He was, nevertheless, an accomplished writer; and in his other works where he was not bound by the task of literal translation he wrote well in a very colorful and clear Russian of his time. Gennadius distinguished himself among the contemporary Russian prelates by his friendliness to the Latin West. In some ways he frankly admitted this tendency, and he may be numbered among the earliest Russian Westernizers who wanted to transplant from the West many things which they considered useful. Unquestionably Gennadius was one of the outstanding religious leaders of his day, and to him must be given great credit for combating the heretical sect of Judaizers.

In assessing the importance of the Strigolniks and the Judaizers, the two major Russian Nonconformist groups of the fourteenth and fifteenth centuries, it may be said that while both arose in opposition to the Established Church, they were not equally "protestant" in character. The Strigolniks may rightly be called "the first Russian protestants," for they protested against abuses within the Established Church and attempted to recapture the simplicity of the Primitive Church. Although they were persecuted and suppressed for their Nonconformity, they took a stand which represented a constructive criticism of the existing order. On the other hand, the Judaizers conducted a campaign of subversive activity within the Church. As a matter of fact, Dimitri Gerasimov, a Russian scholar and diplomat contemporary with Gennadius, observed the rise of the Reformation and did consider the Judaizers to be Russian "protestants." It now seems evident, however, that these heretics were not interested primarily in reforming the Christian Church in Russia. Rather, their tactics and their program were calculated to supplant and to destroy the Church. The Judaizers, therefore, may be thought of from a Christian point of view as destructive critics of the Church.

III.

THE JOSEPHITES AND THE NONPOSSESSORS

In the controversy among Russian Church leaders over what action to take in suppressing the Judaizers, there appeared for the first time in open conflict the two opposing forces which culminated in the great schism of the Russian Church two centuries later. The leader of one of the factions was Saint Joseph of Volokolamsk, who drew to him the supporters and admirers of Gennadius and developed a severe and rigid doctrinal position of far-reaching significance. The other leader, Saint Nilus of Sora, who together with his followers came to be called the Nonpossessors, represented a more moderate and tolerant point of view. The schism of the seventeenth century cannot be understood apart from the background of Saint Joseph and the Josephites and Saint Nilus and the Nonpossessors.

Before studying the lives and works of these two significant characters, however, one should have in mind some important circumstances in Russian history. When the last Greek primate, Isidore, came to Moscow in 1437 to rule the Russian Church, the Byzantine Empire was dying; and the last Palaeologos was trying to escape the Turkish menace with the help of the Latin West. In the hope of gaining Western aid, the Greeks submitted to the pope by signing the act of union with the Roman Church in 1439 at Florence. Although the grand duke of Moscow had tried to dissuade Isidore from going to Italy for the conferences on reunion, Isidore went anyway and took a large delegation with him. At Florence he joined with the other Greek Church leaders in signing the act of union and was rewarded for it with being made a cardinal.

When Isidore finally returned to Moscow in 1441 to proclaim the act of union with Rome, the Muscovite Church leaders heard his announcement with indignation and horror. Believing that he had shamefully betrayed the Orthodox Church, the Russian bishops had Isidore arrested, very quickly deposed him as a heretic, and appointed Saint Jonas, a native prelate, in his place. The Russian churchmen detested the Latins, whom they considered heretics; and they proceeded to break communion with the Greeks when they joined the Roman Church. The Russians interpreted the fall of Constantinople to the Turks in 1453 as a divine punishment of the Greeks for their betrayal of Orthodoxy. Furthermore, the belief spread in Russia that after the fall of Byzantium, Moscow was its rightful successor and that the ruler of Moscow was the true heir of the Byzantine emperors.

Ivan III, a crafty sovereign who reminds us strongly of his contemporary Louis XI of France, ascended the Russian throne in 1462 and embraced the view that his role was that of successor to the Byzantine emperors. He subjugated the great republic of Novgorod in 1478, and two years later he abolished the payment of tribute to the Tartars and formally proclaimed complete Russian independence. In 1472 Ivan had married Princess Sophia Palaeologos, daughter of Thomas, despot of Morea and brother of the two last Byzantine emperors, John VIII and Constantine XI, and adopted the Byzantine coat of arms and court ceremonies. Thus through the independent stand of the Russian Orthodox Church, the achieving of Russian independence, and the consummating of a strategic marriage, Ivan III established Russia as the successor to Byzantium; and Moscow took the place of Constantinople. To justify this new assumption of authority, Russia — the new Byzantium — needed the support of a theological system. Saint Joseph of Volokolamsk probably did more than any other single theologian to provide a doctrinal justification for the new destiny of Russia.[1]

THE JOSEPHITES

Saint Joseph was born to the noble family of Sanin in 1440, and he experienced early the call to the religious life. Trained in the monastic virtues by Saint Paphnutius, abbot of Borovsk, the young Sanin was professed in 1460. Like Bernard of Clairvaux before him, Saint Joseph persuaded his parents and his brothers to follow him to the cloister. When in 1477 Saint Joseph succeeded Saint Paphnutius as the abbot of Borovsk, he tried immediately to increase the severity of the rule; but he met no sympathy within the community toward this step. Discouraged, he resigned the abbacy within one year and left the monastery in order to find a more austere community. After a one year's pilgrimage, Saint Joseph found a rule that appealed to him; this was the rule observed in a northern house, Kirilo-Belozersky monastery, founded in 1397 by Saint Cyril, abbot of Simonovsky monastery at Moscow and a disciple of Saint Sergius of Radonezh. Saint Joseph introduced this rule into his own monastery, which he established near Volokolamsk; and within a few years the new abbey prospered and soon numbered over one hundred brothers.

Life in Volokolamsk monastery was very strict, involving long vigils, severe fasts, hard work, and serious study. Like the Western Cluniacs, Saint Joseph loved fine buildings and long and magnificent services. He was a good preacher, and he did not shrink from contact with the world; indeed he looked for it. For him the monasteries were centers of religious culture, schools of spirituality, which radiated light and love around them. Saint Joseph acted as a spiritual director to several princes and nobles, advised prelates, and often intervened in public affairs to settle quarrels and conflicts of every kind. A man of great abilities and learning, and possessed of an iron will, Saint Joseph soon became recognized as a religious leader.

At the time of the contest with the Judaizers, Saint Gennadius requested Saint Joseph's help in overcoming these heretics and put him at the head of his own supporters. Against the Judaizers, Saint Joseph wrote his celebrated treatise *Prosvetitel* [2] (*The En-*

lightener), a very significant work. *The Enlightener* presents an able defense of Christianity in the light of the arguments of Judaism and gives the best-known description of the Judaizing heresy. Saint Joseph was well read, and he knew the Bible and the patristic writings particularly well. In *The Enlightener* alone he quoted more than forty Church Fathers, and Saint John Damascene seems to have been his particular favorite. While he was an able logician and dialectian, Saint Joseph unfortunately lacked a critical approach to his sources. For him all the writings that circulated in the ecclesiastical milieu and were approved by the ancient bishops were of the same value. He would defend the obscure Nikon the Montenegrin with the same zeal as he would the Bible, and doubts of the veracity of the obscure Father were to Saint Joseph as sinful as those concerning the Bible. Even the nomocanon, the Byzantine canon law, which was full of secular matters, seemed to him as sacrosanct as the dogmatic decrees of the general councils. The last four chapters of *The Enlightener,* where Saint Joseph discussed the measures to be taken against the heretics, produced many discussions and dissensions in the Russian Church. He demanded the severest laws against the heretics, specifying that they should be excommunicated and delivered to the civil authorities to be burned alive. He justified the severest kind of punishment for the Judaizers on the basis that they were not, strictly speaking, Christian heretics but rather apostates from Christianity. Fully realizing the strength of the secret organization of the Judaizers and their outward conformity to the Church, Saint Joseph demanded a diligent search for the heretics and a long probation period for those who repented.

Besides *The Enlightener,* Saint Joseph left also a rule of the monastic life and several other writings. While he rejected the practice of individual monks' holding property, Saint Joseph approved fully the possession of landed estates by the monasteries. He criticized sharply the monastic custom of his age which allowed wealthy people to retire to monasteries in their old age. Such older people were professed nominally; and they lived in the abbeys in every comfort, retaining the right to use their wealth as they pleased, providing that it should pass to the community after their death. This system, which had begun already in Kievan Russia, became very widespread, so that eventually hardly anyone was professed unless he brought with him a large donation. A very few communities accepted poor novices and then only as lay brothers for a lifetime term. Usually the monasteries employed numerous serfs for menial tasks. The Russian monks of that period lived more as did the Oxford and Cambridge dons before the obligation of celibacy was relaxed than as members of a strict religious order. Saint Joseph reformed these loose customs, yet he approved the possession of corporate property and the custom of demanding a donation before professing a novice. He looked upon the monasteries as schools and nurseries for prelates; therefore he favored great and wealthy communities which would attract many novices from the nobility and gentry. The wealthy community was able to present many candidates for episcopal consecration and to spread widely monastic influence. Saint Joseph believed that the prelates — bishops and abbots — must intervene in public affairs as a matter of course. Continuous collaboration between the Church and the State was, to his way of thinking, absolutely necessary for the well-being of both. Saint Joseph greatly helped Ivan III to strengthen his authority, but he opposed the grand duke resolutely when he tried to reduce monastic property for the benefit of the State. Such an attempt he considered sacrilegious.

Volokolamsk monastery quickly became a nursery of bishops. The successor of Saint Joseph in the abbacy, Daniel, became in due course the Russian primate. Several of his monks occupied diocesan sees; and pupils and supporters of Saint Joseph, called Josephites, ruled the Russian Church for a long time and mightily influenced it. Austere, well-organized, liturgically correct, Volokolamsk monastery failed, nevertheless, to become a center of mystical life and evangelical virtues. Too much attention was paid to externals — vigils, fasts, elaborate singing, scrupulous observance of rites and ceremonies — while mental prayer and spiritual reading were neglected. Like Saint Joseph himself, the Josephites read widely but uncritically, considering the Bible, the Fathers, and the nomocanon equally sacrosanct and opposing any attempt to discriminate between them. The Josephites were, in fact, fundamentalists of the most extreme type.

THE NONPOSSESSORS

Opposed to Saint Joseph and his ideology were Saint Nilus of Sora and his disciples, who became known as the Elders of the Volga or the Nonpossessors. This group voiced their views for the first time at the Moscow council in 1503, which was convened to condemn the Judaizers. While the Josephites insisted upon the severe punishment of the Judaizers or even their complete extermination, the Nonpossessors stood for religious toleration. Paisius Yaroslavov, one of the most attractive figures in Russian monastic history, first headed the Nonpossessors. Professed at a monastery near the White Lake beyond the Volga, Paisius quickly became known all over Russia for the saintliness of his life. Ivan III, who admired Paisius, offered him the abbacy of the greatest Muscovite monastery, that of the Holy Trinity, which was founded by Saint Sergius of Radonezh in the fourteenth century.[3] The grand duke wanted to reform the Holy Trinity monastery and to restore it to its former high spiritual level, but Paisius was to remain as head of the monastery for only three years (1479–1482). Soon after he began his work of reform, the community, which was made up largely of retired princes and nobles, rebelled against Paisius and even threatened to murder him if he persisted in his reforming zeal. Rather than give way, Paisius resigned the abbacy; and when, two years later, Ivan III offered him the Russian primacy he, like Saint Sergius before him, refused the honor.

Saint Nilus of Sora succeeded Paisius as leader of the Nonpossessors. Saint Nilus, according to some writers a scion of the noble house of Maikov, which gave to Russia several illustrious men, was professed at Kirilov monastery under Paisius. After his profession, Nilus went to Constantinople, the Holy Land, and Mt. Athos to study the monastic life. Returning to Russia, he attended the first Moscow council against the Judaizers. Nilus visited Saint Gennadius of Novgorod in 1490, but in 1503 he opposed the severe punishment of the Judaizers at the Moscow council and protested against monastic landowning. Paisius joined Saint Nilus in his protest, which was backed by Ivan III, who was eager to secularize at least a part of the monastic estates. Saint Nilus asserted that it was most unbecoming for monks to possess landed property. He held that since monks deny the world and its entanglements, they ought to avoid great estates which would involve them in the affairs of this world and corrupt them. He insisted that monks should live in poverty and evangelic simplicity, maintaining themselves by their own exertions. On these grounds Saint Nilus objected to the founding of large monasteries in populous districts or in cities. Monks, he said, should live retired lives in remote places and be supported not by endowments but by their own labor. Saint Nilus recommended to the monks the sketic form of the religious life which flourished at Mt. Athos. In sketes the monks lived together in small groups, not exceeding twelve persons. Their superior was also their spiritual director, or starets. Saint Nilus advised his monks to use their free time for a diligent and critical study of the Bible and of the Fathers. He prescribed mental prayer as a regular exercise and recommended certain works to undertake, particularly the spiritual direction of the faithful.

In his controversy with the Josephites, Saint Nilus admitted the duty of the Church to excommunicate the apostates and the heretics. He also admitted the necessity in certain circumstances of giving them up to the State for some punishment, but he advocated clemency as more becoming to Christians. In any case he resolutely opposed capital punishment. Saint Nilus taught quite uncompromisingly that the human conscience must be free and that none should be persecuted for his religious views. In that he was well in advance of his age, and the intolerant Josephites were simply unable to understand him. They suspected his very Orthodoxy. A long struggle between the Josephites and the Nonpossessors, which began in 1503, ended eventually in the utter defeat of the Nonpossessors. It might be said that the Josephites and their epigoni reigned supreme in the Russian Church until the patriarch Nikon evicted them. Then they left the Church, carrying with them millions of followers, who formed the great Russian schism or Raskol.

Saint Nilus stated his principles in a charming letter to a monk named Innocent:

" I write to you now about myself because your love for God makes me foolish enough to write to you about my life. When you lived with me in the monastery you learned how I avoided every contact with the world and how I tried, unsuccessfully, alas, to live according to the Divine Writ and tradition of the Holy Fathers. We must live not casually but according to the Scriptures. I left the monastery for the benefit of my soul. . . . I went to Palestine and wandered for a while. Coming back, I built a cell outside the monastery and lived there for a time. Leaving the monastery again, I live at present at this remote place, well known to you, which is agreeable to me. I study now the Bible, the Lord's commandments, commentaries on them and the apostolic writings. I read also the lives and instructions of the Holy Fathers. I meditate over the pages which I read. I write down everything which I find God-inspired and useful to my soul. In this way I educate myself and find how to live rightly. When I am unable to find any advice in the Scriptures upon the task to perform, I postpone my decision until I find such an instruction. I never dare to act solely according to my private judgment and self-will. To all men who love me I give the same advice." [4]

In his rule of the sketic life, Saint Nilus left a very fine spiritual treatise full of instructions on mental prayer and the attainment of virtues. While Saint Joseph filled his rule with many details of monastic administration and discipline, he said relatively little about prayer. Saint Nilus, on the other hand, made prayer the principal subject of his treatise. Influenced undoubtedly by the Hesychasts of Mt. Athos, a school of mystics, who devoted themselves to contemplation of Deity, Saint Nilus taught that mental prayer, particularly the prayer of Jesus, is superior to vocal prayer. External works, he said, mean little or nothing without inner perfection. None can attain this perfection unless he masters himself first, for inner perfection consists in mastering imagination, emotions, and thoughts and then subjecting them to the service of God. In externals, ecclesiastical architecture, ritual, and music Saint Nilus liked extreme simplicity, similar to that of the Latin Carthusians or Cistercians. He stood mainly for the same ideals as Saint Bernard did a few centuries earlier. Saint Nilus died in 1508.[5] With him and Saint Joseph of Volokolamsk we begin to see in the theology of the Russian Church original thought which is truly Russian.

In their early stages of development neither the Josephites nor the Nonpossessors could be considered " Nonconformists " in the sense of separating from the Orthodox Church. Each fostered ideals antithetical to the other, however; and each must have considered the other to be lacking in conformity to basic Christian principles and practices. With the passing of the years the Josephites more and more set themselves up as " Orthodox " par excellence; but when the deep cleavage between the conflicting elements in the Russian Church finally came to decisive issue, the Josephites were put out as schismatic and " Nonconformist." Although the Nonpossessors lost in their struggle with the Josephites, it now appears that the followers of Saint Nilus were, after all, more nearly in accord with basic principles of the Orthodox Church than were their adversaries.

IV.

THE GREAT RUSSIAN SCHISM

After the deposition of Metropolitan Barlaam in 1521 the Josephites captured the Russian primacy and held it firmly in their hands. The Josephites represented a curious mixture of extreme ritualism combined with austere puritanism, to which no exact parallel was known in the West. The most extreme fundamentalists, the Josephites believed not only in the literal divine inspiration of the Bible but they professed that the Holy Ghost inspired as well the ecumenical councils, the Fathers of the Church, the liturgical writers, and the compilers of the canon law. Everything received by the Church and approved by its synods they held as sacrosanct as the Bible itself. The Josephites altogether failed to distinguish between divine and human elements in the Bible and ecclesiastical literature and to find out what is eternal and obligatory for all times and places and what is temporary and confined to a particular age and people. The Josephites naturally rejected any idea of doctrinal development; Orthodoxy consisted for them in the unquestioning acceptance of the ecclesiastical tradition. Any doubt about the correctness of interpretation of the Bible by certain Fathers or councils they considered blasphemous.

The Josephite piety consisted in the scrupulous observance of complicated rites and external asceticism, long vigils, and severe fasts. They approved works of charity and passive and uncritical devotional reading. They loved large, overdecorated churches, splendid vestments, and large choirs, but they cared little for meditation over the Scripture or for mental prayer. The Josephites were fervent nationalists, and they were not greatly concerned about the catholicity of the Church. Unlike the Gallicans, who never quite succeeded in their struggle with Rome, the Josephites easily achieved complete independence of the Russian Church from Constantinople. The Josephites became the foremost champions of the " third Rome " theory which exalted the Russian Church and Muscovy and looked upon all other Orthodox Churches and nations as insignificant and suspect in the very purity of their faith. The Josephites helped to create the new Russian monarchy based on the Byzantine tradition of *rex sacerdos*. For a long time the boyars, led by the numerous princes of the house of Rurik, fought against the rising Muscovite autocracy so contradictory to the Kievan ideas. The boyars nearly succeeded in limiting it for a time in the beginning of the seventeenth century, but ultimately they failed. The pressing needs of the Russian state demanded a strong central power, and the Russian masses frankly preferred a benevolent despot to the selfish rule of the aristocratic oligarchy.

Concealed within the Josephite ideology were grave dangers. It led toward a formalistic and pharisaical religion in a static state. If the Josephites had been left unchecked, they would have accomplished in due course the separation of the Russian patriarchate from the Orthodox Church and in the creation of a new purely national Church similar to that of the Armenians. The notions of the Church, nation, and state would then coincide. It was the liturgical reforms of the patriarch Nikon which finally stopped the process of gradual separation of the Russian patriarchate from the Orthodox Church. The danger of the Josephite ideology was realized, however, long before the time of Nikon.

Already in the fifteenth century many Slavonic-speaking Greek travelers to Moscow found numerous errors, arising from the work of incompetent copyists, in the Russian Scriptures and liturgical books. The Greeks also were distressed to find that the Russian rite began to differ widely from their own and even to contradict it. In a time when ritual uniformity was thought to be essential to the unity of faith, such a divergence inspired serious fears. The Greeks tried many times to impress the Russians with the real need to correct their books and to bring their rites into approximate agreement with those of the Greeks. Saint Maximus the Greek (1480–1556) worked for such an end but met up with disaster.[1] The Council of the Hundred Chapters (1551) solemnly confirmed the Russian translations and rites with only a very few changes. After this pronouncement the difficulty of making any correction increased greatly. Nevertheless an extremely wide variation in the texts of the Russian liturgical books at last forced the Josephites themselves to try to achieve uniformity, and this goal became imperative when the books began to be printed.

The first Russian printed books appeared in the reign of Ivan IV, and the printing of religious books continued under the patriarchs Job and Hermogen from 1598 to 1610, when most of the Russian liturgical books were published. The printing was badly organized. Instead of printing only after selecting the best Slavonic manuscripts and comparing them with the best Greek originals, the editors arbitrarily selected certain Slavonic manuscripts and, without even checking them one against another, started to print. In this way many deplorable and yet easily avoidable errors were perpetuated and sanctified through long use. The publishing program was resumed in 1614 when the Church printing press, which was destroyed by the Poles during an occupation, was restored. As the project got under way again, the extreme fundamentalism of the Josephites was revealed afresh in their persecution of the archimandrite Dionysius.

The Russian bishops entrusted Dionysius, who was superior of the Holy Trinity monastery, and Father Arsenius of the same monastery with the task of editing and publishing the sacramentary, the *Trebnik*. Both of these churchmen were Greek scholars; and they were assigned Rev. Ivan Nasedka, a Moscow priest and Slavonic scholar, as an assistant. Working hard on the project, the editors prepared a good manuscript for publication; but they dared to correct some obvious misprints of the previous editions. Such boldness worked to their undoing, for they were promptly charged with the usual accusations of deliberate corruption of the sacred text and of propagation of heresy. The abbot

Dionysius had ventured only to change a single sentence in the previous edition, but that was enough to raise suspicion. In the prayer for the blessing of water Dionysius discovered the unusual wording: " Now, Lord, thyself, sanctify this water by the Holy Ghost and fire." Unable to find the last word in any ancient Greek or Slavonic manuscript, he simply omitted it. The Josephites thereupon immediately accused him of heretical views on the Holy Ghost. They alleged that he had denied the appearance of the Holy Ghost at Pentecost in the form of fire. The patriarchal locum tenens, Metropolitan Jonas of Krutitsy, assembled a council to discuss the matter. The council found all the editors to be heretics, and they were excommunicated and imprisoned. Several years passed before a new council, convened by Patriarch Philaret, reversed the sentence and acquitted the editors. The patriarch Theophanes of Jerusalem did much to vindicate the editors, and they all were promoted as compensation for their unmerited imprisonment.

Josephite intolerance, nevertheless, continued to flourish unabated, and Metropolitan Jonas himself soon became its victim. Disregarding the already well-established practice of rebaptizing Roman Catholic converts, the metropolitan dared to receive a couple of Roman Catholic Poles after merely anointing them with the holy chrism. The patriarch reprimanded Jonas and called a synod of bishops to study his case. The synod found the Roman Catholics guilty of professing the heresies of the Melchizedekians, Manichaeans, Eunomians, Massalians, and Arians. Still unsatisfied, the synod went on to attribute to the Latins many errors and usages quite alien to them. On the strength of its own findings, the synod decreed that all Western Christians should be rebaptized; and Jonas accepted the synodal decision.

Muscovite exclusiveness was so extreme that the very same synod ordered the rebaptism of all Orthodox Ukrainians and White Russians coming from Poland if there was any possibility that they had been baptized by sprinkling. The Muscovites recognized only baptism by immersion and considered all other forms of the rite to be invalid. Not only were the Muscovites extremely harsh toward the Latins but they classified the Protestants with the Jews and the Moslems as being outside the Christian faith. The proposed marriage between Prince Valdemar of Denmark, son of Christian IV, and Czarevna Irene, daughter of Czar Michael Romanov, failed to take place because of the strong stand of the Russian Church against Protestants. The Russians insisted that Valdemar must be rebaptized before the marriage. In 1644 and 1645 Orthodox and Lutheran Church leaders held several discussions at Moscow to determine whether or not the Lutherans were actually Christians. The Lutherans defended the validity of their baptism, but the Muscovites rejected it. The Russians became convinced that the Lutherans were far more advanced heretics even than the Latins, for they rejected several sacraments, the regular priesthood, apostolic succession, relics, and fasts. In the light of the evidences of Lutheran heresy, the Russians could not believe that their baptism was valid. To the Danes the Russian churchmen seemed to be well read in the sacred Scripture but narrow-minded and quite unable to rise to abstract speculation. It became evident that the Josephites' learning consisted in memorizing a great many texts which they could repeat very cleverly to defend their views. They possessed no method, however, and failed to construct a coherent system of doctrine.

Philaret, who was patriarch of the Russian Church from 1619 to 1633, was the ruling power in both the Russian Church and State; but his immediate successors, Joasaph I and Joseph, could not maintain this exalted position. They enjoyed only the customary title of Great Lord, and they did not sign the imperial decrees nor intervene in public affairs. On the contrary, at this time the State began to interfere with ecclesiastical administration. The impoverished State looked with understandable envy on the tremendous monastic estates, peopled by hundreds of thousands of serfs. The Government wanted to control them and to use their income for its own ends. Until 1649 matters concerning the monastic estates were handled by a special division of the ministry of the Great Palace. The Legal Code of 1649 provided for the organization of a separate department, that of the Monastic Office (Monastyrskii Prikaz), to control the endowments of the Church.

The bishops naturally objected to the State's intervention in the control of the Church's wealth; and although the weak successors of Philaret acquiesced in the new order, it was clear that the first strong patriarch would demand the suppression of the Monastic Office. Already in the days of Hermogen and Philaret, when the patriarchs began to overshadow the czars, a straightforward struggle between them became possible in case of a profound disagreement. It became unavoidable when the State began to intervene in affairs of the Church and to try to use the latter for its own ends.

Under both successors of Philaret the correction and printing of the liturgical books continued without interruption. The editors tried to be as conscientious as possible, but the old difficulties remained. The absence of Greek and Latin scholars was strongly felt; and in order to ease this situation the czar Michael once invited a few learned monks to come to Moscow from Kiev, which then was in Polish territory. The Muscovites, however, did not welcome the Kievan scholars but openly suspected their Orthodoxy and forced them to retire. Finally Father Arsenius Sukhanov, a learned monk and Greek scholar, was sent to the East in 1651 to study the Greek rites and to collect ancient and modern manuscripts and books. A Josephite at heart, Arsenius despised the Greeks and the Syrians, who were slaves of the Moslem sultan. Arsenius found many divergences between the Greek and Muscovite rites; but he attributed them at once to the corruption of Greek Orthodoxy by the Latins and Anglicans who printed their books in the West.

Such was the general situation in the Russian Church when Nikon, metropolitan of Novgorod, ascended the patriarchal throne in 1652. Nikon undoubtedly was the greatest patriarch or primate ever to appear in Russia. He was a Russified Volga Finn, Nikita Minin; and he was born to a peasant family. His childhood under the ferule of a harsh stepmother was painful and even tragic, but it made him a man of iron will. Nikita was a very clever boy, and he quickly took advantage of all the educational opportunities available in his district. Although he wanted to become a monk, his relatives persuaded him to marry and to become a parish priest. Nikita, however, did not remain a secular priest for long. The unexpected death of all his children convinced him that he must accept the call to the monastic life. He persuaded his wife, later an abbess, to take the veil; and he, taking the name of Nikon, became a monk in a remote monastery in Arctic Russia. Czar Alexis met Nikon once at Moscow, where he had come on business, and was greatly impressed with him. After that Nikon's promotion was extremely rapid. He became abbot of Novo-Spassky monastery at Moscow, then metropolitan of Novgorod; and in 1652, while he was still in his early forties, he was made patriarch of all Russia. Once on the patriarchal throne, Nikon decided to speed up the correction of the liturgical books, bringing the Russian rite nearer to that of the Greek. He hardly realized what a dangerous path he was about to take.

Under Nikon's predecessor, Patriarch Joseph, the two Moscow archpriests, Gregory Neronov and the czar's confessor Stephen Vonifatiev, supervised the ecclesiastical publications. Although they were themselves moderate Josephites, they were surrounded by extremists and rabid nationalists, mostly from the provinces. Outstanding among the extreme reactionaries were the archpriests Avvakum of Yurievets,[2] Daniel of Kostroma, and Longin of Murom. Nikon's intention to reform the Russian rites and to change the Russian sign of the cross and the Russian way of singing in order to attain uniformity with the Greeks was blasphemy and heresy to the Josephites. They resolutely opposed the patriarch and declared him a heretic.

The struggle between Nikon, a man of iron will, and the extreme Josephites, led first by Archpriest Neronov and then by Avvakum, began. It was a long, hard, and bitter struggle which broke forever the unity of the Russian Church and originated the great schism, or Raskol. A man more cautious and tactful than Nikon might have been able to accomplish the needed liturgical reforms without raising such a storm. Nikon, although gifted and energetic, was imperious and unbending. He had no use for diplomacy, and he forced his reforms harshly and uncompromisingly on the unwilling clergy and people, driving out of the Church masses of conservative peasants. Nevertheless, in spite of all opposition, Nikon succeeded in his reforms. Czar Alexis, together with prelates, court officers, nobles, and a strong party within the clergy, supported him. Nikon excommunicated his uncompromising adversaries; and they left the Church, led by the archpriest Avvakum, who was a typical extreme Josephite of the age. A son of an insignificant secular priest from Nizhnii Novgorod province, Avvakum was as able and unbending as his adversary, Nikon. As a true Josephite, Avvakum believed that everything Russian was sacred and perfect, needing no change or improvement. Any liturgical reform seemed to him a deliberate corruption of the ancestral faith which had made Russia great, holy, and strong.

Nikon carried out his reforms easily because he was a close personal friend of the czar. Under this favorable relationship the Russian patriarchate in the hands of Nikon reached its zenith of importance and power, but the anticlimax was shortly to follow. With Nikon, the patriarch became once more the great sovereign, received the ambassadors, presided over the council of state (boiarskaia duma), and acted as regent in the absence of the czar. Nikon possessed a magnificent court, a vast income, and concentrated power. Beside the great and imperious patriarch, the meek and quiet czar Alexis looked unimportant. An able administrator and statesman, Nikon was hard and severe with the great nobles. He needlessly humiliated them; and the irritated boyars replied with a well-conceived intrigue which aimed to estrange the czar from the patriarch. Disliking the patriarch personally, the nobles disliked even more his ideology, which insisted on the pre-eminence of the priesthood over the throne. Nikon looked upon the patriarchal power with the eyes of a medieval pope, and this assumption of power not only irritated the nobles but displeased the czar as well. The boyars therefore cherished as their goal the fall of Nikon, who had succeeded in reducing the Monastic Office. They hoped again to control the Church endowments and, taxing them heavily, to reduce the taxation of their own estates. The stage was set, therefore, to overthrow the great patriarch, who faced powerful foes at every hand and had hardly any friends left.

In 1658 the czar and the patriarch reached an impasse in their relations. The czar ceased to trust his friend, and Nikon could not resign himself to this new relationship. Unfortunate attempts of mutual explanation only made the situation worse. Realizing that he could not carry out his reforms without the czar's support, Nikon decided to abdicate and to retire to New Jerusalem monastery, which he had recently founded. Nikon hoped that the czar, grieved by his abdication, would ask him to come back on the condition that he would promise proper obedience. The patriarch carried out his plan to abdicate, but he miscalculated the result. Alexis was certainly astonished with Nikon's move; but he let him go, and the patriarch irrevocably lost his throne. For eight long years the Russian Church was ruled by locum tenens, for Alexis did not know what he should do, whether to depose Nikon officially and appoint a new patriarch by himself or to convene a special council. According to the Russian tradition a patriarch could be deposed only by the council of many bishops, where all other patriarchs should be present or represented. In such a situation all the numerous adversaries of Nikon would, of course, come forward. The Josephites wanted to undo his liturgical reforms, which were approved by the council of Moscow in 1655, insisting that Nikon was an apostate or even an antichrist; and the boyars wanted once more to establish their control over the Church estates. After several unsuccessful efforts to solve the tangle by other means, Alexis decided to risk convening the great council in Moscow in order to depose Nikon and to elect his successor. A clever but utterly unscrupulous Greek adventurer, Paisius, metropolitan of Gaza in Palestine, who was sometimes an Orthodox and sometimes a Uniate, became the czar's chief adviser in the Nikon affair.

The great council met at Moscow in 1667, and the patriarchs Paisius of Alexandria and Macarius of Antioch were present together with all the Russian and many Greek, Serb, Rumanian, and Georgian prelates and a large number of abbots. The council duly deposed Nikon and elected Joasaph II to be his successor. Nevertheless, the council disappointed both the Josephites and the boyars. The council confirmed the reforms of Nikon and excommunicated unreservedly his adversaries; furthermore, it restored to the Church the control of its estates. When the council excommunicated Nikon's adversaries, it formally admitted the existence of the schism, or Raskol, in the Russian Church.[3]

The schism began, as we have seen, in the opposition of certain archpriests, notably Neronov and Avvakum, to Nikon's liturgical reforms. The patriarch, however, succeeded in silencing the opposition; and some of its leaders died. Avvakum was exiled to Siberia, and Archpriest Neronov submitted, receiving permission to celebrate according to the old rite. If Nikon had remained patriarch, the Raskol very probably would have died out gradually just as schismatic movements had died before. Nikon's abdication, however, changed the picture. All the extreme Josephites became greatly excited with what seemed to them a golden opportunity to destroy the Nikonians and definitely to separate the Russian Church from the Greeks, whom they considered corrupt and heretical. Neronov resumed his opposition to Nikon's reforms after the patriarch abdicated, and Avvakum came back from Siberia to aid him. Together they succeeded in interesting several noble ladies, including the wife of the czar, in their plans; and their fervent and unscrupulous propaganda quickly rallied around them many of the clergy and a multitude of laymen attached to the old ways.

The Raskolniks accused the Orthodox, whom they called the Nikonians, of numerous heresies because they began to cross themselves with three fingers instead of two, to sing " Alleluia " thrice instead of twice, to transcribe the name of our Lord differently, and to carry out other innovations. To create a schism in the Church over such small matters may appear ridiculous today, but the excommunicated Raskolniks felt that important issues were at stake. They believed, and rightly up to a point, that rites reflect different interpretations of the cardinal Christian dogmas dealing with the blessed Trinity, the nature of our Lord, and the doctrine of the Church. The Raskolniks therefore accused the Orthodox of adopting such heresies as Arianism, Macedonianism, Nestorianism, and papism. To justify the new rite as a step necessary to halt the gradual alienation of the Russians from the Greeks was to take a stand ridiculous in the eyes of the Raskolniks. They believed that the Greeks were heretics, who said their Mass according to books printed by papists in Italy, and they were even doubtful of the validity of Greek baptism. They felt, therefore, that a separation from the Greeks would be a good thing.

The doctrine of the Raskol quickly crystallized as a further development of the third Rome theory. The Raskolniks believed that Moscow, the third Rome, like Rome and Constantinople, had become heretical. Thus the last Christian kingdom in the world had disappeared. Russia had been corrupted by Antichrist and Moscow had become his camp. The czar and the Orthodox prelates were his servants, and they were to be avoided by all true believers. The Raskolniks accordingly awaited the imminent end of the world; and they, like the early Christians, lived in the expectation of the Second Advent. They expected the end of the world in 1669, and they neglected their businesses and spent their time in fasting and prayer to prepare for the event. But nothing happened. New calculations were made, and 1699 was proclaimed to be the year of the Last Judgment. This dreaded year duly arrived and proved to be quite an ordinary one. Again nothing happened except that Czar Peter the Great, son of Alexis, returned to Moscow from abroad in an unusual way. He entered his capital with complete disregard for the ancient ceremonial, which prescribed visits to shrines and churches as a thanksgiving.

Peter's blasphemies, coarseness, and frank contempt for the old ways convinced the Raskolniks that he was the Antichrist predicted in the Bible. Assuming that Peter was the Antichrist, the extremist Raskolniks began to think of ways to save themselves from falling into his hands. Some fled to the impenetrable forests of northern Russia, but many decided that the best way to avoid satanic seduction was to perish. While some of the most fanatical Raskolniks, including Archpriest Avvakum, were burned at the stake in the reign of Peter's elder brother Theodore, Peter himself did not burn the schismatics. Disappointed in failing to obtain from him the crown of martyrdom, the fanatics decided to burn themselves in order to escape the satanic seduction to apostatize. Several thousands of the fanatics in paroxysms of mass hysteria resigned themselves to be burned to death by special preachers, who collected them into empty barns, locked them in, and burned them. With much labor and difficulty, Peter stopped the practice of mass self-destruction, but the episode made him still more contemptuous of religion. After the most uncompromising schismatics perished in their self-inflicted auto-da-fé, the remaining moderate majority was confronted with a pressing problem: How could they establish a *modus vivendi* with the sinful world?

V.

THE PRIESTISTS

When the Raskolniks, or Old Believers as they were often styled, began to believe that Antichrist was reigning in the world and that he had made the Russian Church his temple, they began almost immediately to experience a grave difficulty. Although the Raskolniks considered their society to be the only true Church of Christ in existence, not a single bishop left the Orthodox Church to join them. This circumstance gave rise to serious complications. Priests ordained before the time of Nikon's abdication and the beginning of the Raskol and who had joined the schismatic group administered sacraments to the Raskolniks, but these priests could not be expected to live forever. Since there were no bishops to ordain new priests, inevitably the time would come when there would be no priests left. In order to delay this dreaded time, Avvakum allowed the Raskolniks to accept as true priests anyone who celebrated according to the old rites without inquiring when they were baptized or ordained. This expedient delayed the ultimate crisis for several decades, but the time finally came when all those priests, supposedly baptized and ordained before 1667, died out. Some solution of the problem of the ministry had to be found at any cost, and two solutions were proposed.

The moderates among the Raskolniks refused to agree that the priesthood and the sacraments should disappear altogether. They admitted that the Russian Church had fallen into the "Nikonian heresy," but they insisted that its orders remained valid just as orders remained valid in the hands of men guilty of lesser heresies. According to these moderates, any Nikonian priest, once he abjured his heresy, became a true priest and was able to dispense valid sacraments. The Raskolniks who lived in central Russia and who had been accustomed for centuries to sacramental and priestly Christianity accepted the solution of the moderates. They came to be called the Popovtsy — the Priestists. The Priestists had some secret centers in the remote parts of Russia. The first center abroad was formed during the regency of Sophia, sister of Peter the Great. At this time the Raskolniks were severely persecuted, and some of them fled to Poland, where they were tolerated. In Poland, near the Russian frontier, the fugitives founded the first Priestist center abroad, the village Vetka. Two priests, Cosma and Stephen, became leaders of the colony; and their successor, priest Joseph, persuaded his flock to build a permanent church and to settle down instead of awaiting interminably the Second Advent. Theodosius, successor of Joseph, consecrated the new church, which remained for a long time the only church of the Raskolniks. He also was the first Raskolnik to admit the priests ordained after 1666 as priests. Large donations from all the provinces of Russia began to pour into the chests of the Vetka community, which prospered exceedingly. The wealth and influence of Vetka, however, worked toward its undoing. The Russian Government became alarmed with the fear that Vetka, well manipulated by foes of Russia, could produce new schisms and new disorders within Russia. In 1733 the Russian authorities invited the inhabitants of Vetka to return to Russia; and when they refused to do so, the Russian troops, commanded by Colonel Suitin, with utter disregard for Polish sovereignty crossed the frontier, burned all the Vetka buildings, and captured its 40,000 inhabitants. The indomitable Raskolniks managed to come back, however, and to restore Vetka once more. The community was finally destroyed in 1764 in the reign of Catherine II; and with the destruction of Vetka, the center of the Priestist movement was transferred successively to Starodubie, Irgiz, and Moscow.

The Priestists very quickly subdivided into several *tolki,* or sects, over the manner in which Orthodox priests should be received into their communities. It had been traditional for the Eastern Church to receive heretics in different ways. Some heretics were rebaptized since their original baptism was considered to be invalid. Some were received through chrismation only, the Eastern form of confirmation, and a few were received solely with penance. At the beginning of the Raskol when the hatred of the separatists toward the Russian Church was at its peak, the Raskolniks usually rebaptized the Russian priests who joined them. Furthermore, to preserve their priestly character, the Priestists rebaptized their converted ministers fully vested. In the eighteenth century, when the sectarian hatred had somewhat abated, Alexander the Deacon began to teach a bold doctrine. He asserted that the Russian Church was in no way heretical but that it only had adopted some unbecoming rites, which were contradictory to the old tradition. Once a convert promised to follow the ancient rite, Alexander reasoned, he should be received with no further ado. To rebaptize the priests and then to receive the sacraments from them was absurd, for if the priests needed to be rebaptized, they were not Christians and therefore could not have been real priests. Since no recognized bishop was available, Alexander thought that it was equally absurd to reconfirm the converted priests.

A council of the Priestists was convened at Moscow in 1779 to settle the matter, and this council abolished the rebaptizing of Orthodox converts and ordered their reception with chrismation only. This decree failed to satisfy the followers of Alexander, however, and several of them decided to submit to the Orthodox Church on certain conditions which they believed to be just. In 1783 a Priestist monk, Nicodemus, petitioned the Holy Synod on behalf of his group 1,500 strong. They wanted to join the Russian Church provided that the excommunication of the Raskolniks decreed by the council of Moscow in 1667 would be repealed and that they would be allowed to use the ancient rite. The synod granted the request, and the group returned to the Orthodox Church. Thereafter several Priestists, led by the archpriest Andrew Ivanov, joined the Russian Church in 1788, forming the so-called Edinovertsy parishes. Several Priestist monasteries also submitted to the Russian Church, and in 1800 the Holy Synod promulgated special canons which regularized the position of the

Edinovertsy within the Russian Church.

Just as was the case with the Ukrainian Uniates in the Roman Church, the Edinovertsy were looked upon for a long time as second-class Orthodox Christians. They were tolerated, however; and the Orthodox view became established that it was unchristian to keep people outside the Church just because they clung to the ancient rite. The Edinovertsy gradually spread, and the conversion of several religious communities notably strengthened their position. In the reign of Nicholas I (1825–1855), who was anxious to strengthen the Russian Church as a bulwark of monarchy, every inducement and even an outright pressure were applied to the Priestists to encourage them to join the Edinovertsy. In 1851 the latter possessed already 179 parishes of their own. They were, nevertheless, not allowed to have their own bishop but were made subject to the Orthodox prelates. In 1900 the Edinovertsy possessed 300 parishes. Their subsequent growth was fast. On the eve of the revolution in 1917 they accounted for nearly 2,000 parishes scattered all over the Russian empire. Each diocese numbered at least thirty Edinovertsy parishes[1]; and considering that these parishes usually were large and populous, the membership may have included as many as two million people in 1917. In these parishes services were celebrated according to the very solemn and beautiful ancient unreformed rites, and several bishops preferred these old rites to the newer reformed ritual. In 1918 the patriarch Tikhon consecrated the Edinovertsy archpriest S. Shleev as bishop of Okhta, and since that time the Edinovertsy have had their own bishops. The present patriarch Alexis is very friendly to them, and hopes are expressed that many more Priestists may join their ranks.

While the followers of Alexander the Deacon rejoined the Orthodox Church, the majority of the Priestists continued to receive the Russian priests through chrismation. Rogozhsky monastery at Moscow, founded in the eighteenth century to bury at its cemetery the Priestist dead, became their chief center; and for decades they experienced no difficulty in finding their priests among the Russian clergy. With the passing of the seventeenth century, the penal laws against the Raskolniks became largely inoperative; and beginning with the reign of Catherine II (1762–1796) the Russian Government took pride in its religious toleration. The Priestists were left alone, and the Orthodox priests who joined them were not disturbed. Since the social and economic position of the Russian clergy was highly unsatisfactory during the entire eighteenth century, there was always a good number of the Russian priests willing to join the Raskolniks. The semi-Protestant or freethinking imperial Government suspected the clergy of anti-Government leanings, and besides looked upon the Orthodox Church as a survival of the barbarian age to be kept in its place and to be used to inculcate obedience to the State among the masses. The clergy were ruined by heavy taxation, and the members were forcibly conscripted into the armed forces or made serfs. The social status of the clergy was low; and many priests, disliking the enslavement of the Church by the State and abhorring the protestantizing or deistic tendencies of the rulers, joined the Priestists quite easily or even eagerly.

The circumstances that enabled the Priestists to enjoy a slow but steady growth changed, however, with the accession of Nicholas I (1825–1855). Nicholas disliked the Raskolniks and the sectarians alike since he believed them to be breeding grounds for political radicalism, as they sometimes were. At this time, therefore, the penal laws again began to be applied to the Nonconformists with growing severity. On the other hand, a rapid succession of decrees greatly improved the position of the Orthodox clergy, which was assimilated into the gentry. When the lot of the Orthodox clergy became greatly improved, the Priestists began to experience more and more difficulty in finding priests to staff their parishes and monasteries. The Priestist position was weakened further by the Government policy of closing down monasteries and parishes and arresting Nonconformist clergy; thus within two decades the shortage of Priestist clergy became desperate.

The Priestists solved their problem by creating their own hierarchy, a move which they had attempted unsuccessfully many times before. Now they were determined to go through with the plan of finding an Orthodox prelate outside of Russia who would consent to consecrate bishops for them, and Nicholas' legislation forced them to act energetically. Realizing very well that Nicholas I never would allow the establishment of a new Priestist hierarchy in his empire, the family of Gromov, merchant princes of St. Petersburg, took the lead in deciding to establish the new hierarchy outside of Russia. The Gromovs selected the small monastery of Bela Krynitsa in the Austrian province of Bukovina, which housed a small community of Priestist descendants of fugitives from Russia, as the seat for the new hierarchy. Once the Gromovs had selected this location they supplied two Priestist monks, Paul Velikodvorsky and Gerontius Kolpakov, with large funds and sent them to obtain the Austrian imperial decree creating an episcopal see for the Priestists residing in Austrian dominions. After this requested decree was issued in 1844, the next step was to find a prelate willing to consecrate the Priestist bishops. Armed with the Austrian decree, Velikodvorsky and his assistant, monk Alimpius, went to the Middle East looking for a suitable prelate. The two monks were very happy to discover that the Greeks baptized by immersion and that they kept severe fasts and many ritual observances; and they decided, therefore, to try to obtain their hierarch from the Greeks.

At last the two monks found a suitable prelate in Constantinople. He was Ambrosius, metropolitan of Bosna-Sarajevo, a son of a Rumelian (southern Bulgarian) priest, who was a Greek. He was born in 1791 and made bishop in 1835, but the Turkish Government soon expelled him from his diocese because he criticized its policy toward his flock. Since that time Ambrosius had lived in retirement at Constantinople. There Velikodvorsky related to him the Priestist difficulties and requested him to help them. He told Ambrosius that the Priestists were strict Orthodox who were persecuted solely on political grounds. Finally he offered to the prelate the primacy in the new hierarchy. After long hesitation Ambrosius came to the conclusion that he would not be betraying Orthodoxy by accepting Velikodvorsky's offer. He came, therefore, to Bela Krynitsa in 1846, where the Priestists received him with anointing — a most unsuitable proceeding which astonished and annoyed the prelate. In 1847 Ambrosius consecrated Cyril

Timofeev to be his assistant bishop. This consecration of a new
bishop was accomplished just in time to save the new hierarchy,
for within a few months the Austrian Government, giving in to
Russian pressure, arrested Ambrosius, imprisoned him for life in
a Styrian castle, and dissolved Bela Krynitsa as a monastery.

The Russian Government failed, however, to destroy the Priestist hierarchy. Cyril, who succeeded Ambrosius, reopened Bela
Krynitsa within a few years and obtained final legalization of the
Priestist hierarchy in the Hapsburg dominions. Cyril consecrated
a few bishops for the Priestists in Turkey and Rumania, where
their position was quickly regularized. In 1849, Cyril dared to
consecrate Sophronius of Simbirsk, a well-read peasant, as the
first Priestist bishop for the Russian empire. Within a short time
a second bishop, Anthony, was consecrated for Moscow itself,
and within a decade the Priestists possessed in Russia twelve
bishops and a multitude of priests. Ten regular dioceses were organized in Russia, and the Priestist dependence on the Russian
clergy ended.

After the creation of their own hierarchy, the Priestists lived
quietly. The only serious trouble which they experienced was
produced by the encyclical letter "Okruzhnoe Poslanie," composed in 1862 by Hilarion Egorov-Ksenov, Priestist divine, and
signed by Humphrey (Onutril), locum tenens of Bela Krynitsa,
and other Russian prelates. This encyclical repeated forcefully the
old arguments of Alexander the Deacon and Nicodemus and
even suggested reconciliation with the Russian Church.[2] Indeed,
Humphrey himself with two other bishops and many priests
afterward joined the Russian Church, but they were received only
as monks because the Russian synod declared Ambrosius' ordinations invalid.

The more radical Priestists opposed the encyclical as they had
opposed Alexander the Deacon in the past. The encyclical divided the Priestists into two groups: Okruzhniki-pro and Neo-
kruzhniki-con. While in the eighteenth century the adversaries of
Alexander the Deacon had formed the majority of the Priestists,
in the nineteenth century they were a minority. With the progress of time the Priestists formed two provinces — one of Mos-

cow, which included all Russian dioceses, and a second of Bela Krynitsa, which included all the dioceses outside Russia, chiefly in Rumania and Turkey. The Priestist prelate Yuzov considered the number of the Priestists in the '8o's of the last century to be three million. By the decree of April 17, 1905, the Priestists received complete freedom of worship, and their churches in Rogozhskoe were restored to them on December 5, 1905.

The Priestists held a council in Moscow in 1906, hoping to unite their two factions; but they were unable to achieve union. They survived the Revolution almost as well as the Orthodox; and in 1926 they had twenty-one bishops in Russia and five in Rumania, besides three Neokruzhniki prelates.[3] According to a statement given on November 16, 1946, by Rev. S. Evans, editor of *Religion and the People,* in his address to the London meeting of St. John Damascene Society, the Priestists once more hold Rogozhskoe, their center in Moscow. The present archbishop of Moscow, Irenarch Parfenov, has spoken of a Priestist plan to unite both their provinces and to transfer their primatial see from Bela Krynitsa to Moscow. He believes that the Priestists now must be three million strong, nearly all of them Okruzhniki, that is, friendly to the Russian Church.

The occupation of Bukovina by the Red Army in 1940 caused Metropolitan Silvanus and his monks to flee from Bela Krynitsa. The abbey was occupied by the Soviet authorities, who, it is alleged, took many rare books, manuscripts, and icons to Moscow museums. The metropolitan died while away and another was elected. During the reoccupation of Bukovina by the Rumanians, however, the community returned to Bela Krynitsa.

The well-known French historian of the Russian Raskol, M. P. Pascal, has published some most valuable information about the present state of the Priestists in his article " L'Église des Vieux-Croyants d'après ses calendriers " in *Russie et Chrétienté* (July–December, 1949, Paris).

The Priestists are governed now by the Archiepiscopal Council, presided over by the archbishop of Moscow and of All Russia, Irenarch Parfenov. The council has, besides him, six members: Gerontius, bishop of Yaroslavl and Kostroma; Joseph, bishop of

Kishinev and Odessa; Benjamin, bishop of Kiev and Vinnitsa; Archpriest Basil Korolev, dean of the Priestist cathedral in Moscow; Archpriest Peter Mikheev, rector of Chuvoe-Nareevo; and Cyril Abrikosov, general secretary. Irenarch Parfenov is, as before, archbishop and not yet primate. The General Council of the Priestists is still in preparation. Its first aim will be to transfer from Rumania to Moscow the Priestist primacy. Before 1941 the Priestist primate lived in Bela Krynitsa. After the incorporation of Bukovina into the Soviet Union in 1945, however, the celebrated Bela Krynitsa monastery was closed and the present Priestist primate lives in Galatz.

Archbishop Irenarch Parfenov, a native of Nizhnii Novgorod province, was originally a country priest. He became the bishop of Samara, Ufa, and Ulyanovsk in 1928 and archbishop in 1941. From 1942 to 1947 he ordained about fifty priests and deacons and opened a school for singers and readers. On November 18, 1946, when he was sixty-five years old, he received congratulations from the Government. For the first time in three hundred years the Priestists were so honored.

According to the Priestist calendar for 1947, quoted by M. Pascal, there are 50,000 faithful in Moscow and its neighborhood. The magnificent Priestist cathedral, which can accommodate 10,-000 persons, is often full. A bishopric is to be founded in Rostov-on-Don. Churches have been repaired in Nizhnii Novgorod (Gorki) and in Kiev. In Kishinev the Priestless have joined the Priestists, and as a matter of fact during the last few years several Priestless congregations have joined the Priestists in the Soviet Union and elsewhere. Furthermore, there have been some startling innovations among the Priestists. Their publications are now printed according to the new orthography. Their calendar years now are dated from the Nativity of our Lord and not from the creation of the world as previously. The Soviet feasts are introduced into their calendar, and the Soviet patriotism of the Priestists is much stressed. No doubt many Priestists do not approve this new development, but whether they have their own clandestine organization or not none abroad can say.

In their letter to Constantin V, patriarch of Constantinople

(1887-1902), the Priestists stated why they kept aloof from the Russian Church. "The Russian Raskol is not a separation from the Orthodox Church but a protest against the enslavement of the Church by the State, against various Latin and Protestant innovations introduced in the Russian Church by followers of the Protestant thinker Leibnitz and ex-papist Theophanes Prokopovich, against the exclusion of people from the body of the Church and Latinization of the clergy, against the assertion that not people but clergy make the Church, against the anticanonical Church administration."[4] The Greek canonists, however, while fully sympathizing with the Priestists, said: "While the Russian Old Ritualists will be separated from the Russian Church, their hierarchy cannot be recognized as canonical. No autocephalous Church can be in communion with it without breaking its communion with the Russian Church." Otherwise they could be received in their orders.

The validity of the Priestist order as yet has not been recognized by the Russian Church, although several theologians believe that they should be so recognized. The Roman Church recognized the Priestist orders as valid in 1910, when one Priestist clergyman, Fr. Susalev, became Uniate. There is a movement now on foot in the U.S.S.R. which aims to bring the Priestists back to the Russian Church. Certain Priestists who obtained their orders from a Renovator (Living Church) bishop Eustace in 1923 expressed their wish to join the Russian Church and petitioned the patriarch. Archpriest Bogoliubov, however, maintains the old Russian attitude toward the Priestists: Ambrosius, consecrating their first bishops in a highly irregular way, invalidated their orders. They are null and void. The Russian Church alone cannot revalidate them but the Great Council of the entire Orthodox Church could by economy recognize the Priestist orders which derive from Ambrosius. Those derived from the Renovators, however, can never be accepted as valid.[5]

Meanwhile those Priestists who want to join the Orthodox Church could be received as the Edinovertsy. The Old Believer priest, Joseph Pervyi, was received into the Russian Church on May 24, 1947, in Odessa and then reordained by the bishop of

Odessa, Sergius Larin, who, although a Renovator bishop in the past, was received into the Church himself as a layman and re-ordained. Fr. Pervyi was appointed to minister the Kherson Edinovertsy.

The Edinovertsy form a natural bridge between the Orthodox Church and the Raskol. Indeed it could be said that now nearly all Raskolniks are absorbed either in Edinoverie or in the Priest-ist Church, usually called Austrian or Belo-Krynitskaia.[6] Even now Church leaders in Moscow are studying the problem of making the reunion complete.

The Priestless group in the Raskol, however, suffered a more stormy career.

VI.

THE PRIESTLESS

While the moderate Raskolniks accepted the validity of the Russian, Nikonian orders, the extremists flatly rejected them. The Russian Church became for them a heretical body deprived of sacramental grace. Once the pre-Nikonian priests died out, the extremists argued, priesthood is lost forever. With its disappearance, all the sacraments except baptism became inoperative. Avvakum and his fanatical followers laid the foundation for this group of the Raskolniks, called the Bezpopovtsy or the Priestless.

The harsh penal laws passed against the Raskolniks in the reign of Alexis and Theodore and during the regency of Sophia (1682–1689) inspired them with the expectation of the end of the world. Several fanatics appeared among the Raskolniks and urged upon them self-immolation in order to escape the dire danger of being perverted by the artifices of Antichrist and of perishing forever. Many ignorant peasants and artisans responded to this propaganda all over Russia and preferred self-immolation to eternal damnation. Some twenty thousand people burned themselves to death in the seventeenth century after listening to such sermons.[1]

Gradually, however, these extremist views subsided. Peter the Great, a freethinker himself, pitied the ignorant Priestless and allowed them to observe their rites and customs, provided they would pay a special tax, wear a special garb, and not proselytize. Peter's tolerance allowed the Priestless to organize, and they established their center in northern Russia. In the vast Novgorodian lands with their ancient Nonconformist tradition, the shortage of the clergy was permanent. Since time immemorial the northern laymen were accustomed to baptize, to confess their sins to each other, and to bury their own dead. The churches were few and parishes tremendous in extent, and most of the people went to church only on rare occasions. The isolated villagers usually went to the village chapel where the literate laymen conducted on proper days all services allowed to laity.

Priests visited these remote colonies very rarely, sometimes only once in every few years. To these folk the Priestless doctrine and practice was not so shocking and unusual as it was to the Raskolniks of central Russia, who always had lived with the clergy and were accustomed to their ministrations. Besides, the Strigolniks, the Judaizers, and the heretical Nonpossessors had maintained in the north for three centuries the vision of nonpriestly Christianity. Further, Protestant influences filtered in from Sweden and Germany. The Swedes occupied a large part of Novgorodian lands and Novgorod itself in the time of troubles, in the beginning of the seventeenth century. They printed in Stockholm and distributed among the Novgorodians the Lutheran catechism in Slavonic. All these circumstances provided favorable soil in which the Priestless movement could take root.

Macarius, metropolitan of Novgorod, successor of Nikon in the northern capital, sympathized with the Raskolniks and left them undisturbed in his vast diocese. Many Raskolnik extremists came, consequently, to northern Russia to settle there. The great monastery of Solovki, founded by Saint Zosima and Saint Sabbatius in the fifteenth century, provided a good many supporters of the Raskol. This monastery was a great cultural and trading center in the north which exploited the Arctic coast and played an important part in Russian economy. The Solovki monks were much attached to the old rites and refused to accept the new. In 1667 they rose in rebellion against the suggestion of the czar that Archimandrite Joseph be their superior. The Government then sent a strong military force to reduce the abbey which was also a strong fortress. The siege lasted several years until December 23, 1675, during which time the great monastery was stormed in vain. It was betrayed by a monk on January 22, 1676; and most of the monks were killed outright by infuriated soldiers. The rebellious archimandrite Nicanor and twenty-seven others were hanged or cut to pieces. Out of five hundred monks in 1674 only fourteen remained in the monastic prison, when the new archimandrite Macarius, accompanied by a new community, came to Solovki.

During the siege of Solovki a good many monks, however, escaped to the Continent from the island on which the monastery is situated. They became the most uncompromising propagandists of the Raskol. No accommodation with the Nikonian Church was countenanced. The Raskolniks were to have their organization completely independent of that of the Established Church and this organization was to be of the monastic type.

THE SHORE DWELLERS

A monk of Solovki named Ignatius, accompanied by another monk, Cornelius, traveled across the Novgorodian north, spreading the devotion to the old faith. Their propaganda much impressed a lay reader of Shun, Daniel Vikulin, who, with a few other sympathizers, decided to establish a small religious community to perpetuate the old faith. In his design he was greatly helped by Andrew Denisov, of the family of the princes Myshetsky, who came to the north in 1692. Together they founded in 1695 the celebrated Danilovsky monastery on the river Vyg in the province of Olonets, which bordered the Swedish Finland.[2]

Although Daniel Vikulin, a lay reader, was its nominal founder, the monastery owed its fame and prosperity to the brothers Andrew and Simeon Denisov, the greatest of the Priestless divines. In 1706 they also established a convent near by for nuns. Anyone who expressed his wish to follow the ancient rite and to observe the monastic rule was accepted. All the newcomers, excepting the Priestless, naturally were rebaptized. Andrew Denisov, a man of genius, colonized and greatly improved several remote districts of Arctic Russia.

Educated at Moscow and Kiev, where he attended lectures on theology and philosophy, Andrew Denisov was an able scholar and clever controversialist. A monk by conviction, Denisov im-

posed compulsory celibacy upon all men and women who came
to his monastery and convent and their dependencies; but the
rule of compulsory celibacy imposed on the thousands of people
who lived at Vyg colony could not be enforced. The majority of
Denisov's followers were the most convinced and fervent Priestless believers, yet they were quite unable to live in perpetual
chastity. In order to avoid troubles and debauchery, Denisov was
obliged to divide his followers into two groups. The professed
monks and nuns remained in their respective monasteries, but
those who came married and with children were settled in villages around Vyg.

The monastery itself was administered according to Andrew
Denisov's rule, " Ulozhenie," inspired by the monastic ideal of
Saint Joseph of Volokolamsk. The Vyg villages, on the other side,
strongly suggest the Soviet collectivized villages. Vyg was administered by a bolshak, assisted by other officers, all elected by
the *sobor,* or assembly of colonists.[3] Tolerated by Peter the Great
and his successors, Vyg monastery and its numerous dependencies
grew in strength and influence. Vyg sent hunting expeditions as
far as Spitsbergen and Novaya Zemlya, and possessed great fish-
eries on the lake of Onega, cultivated vast lands for farming, and
traded on a large scale with the Russian south. One hundred and
fifty years after its foundation, Vyg still earned nearly 200,000
roubles a year. Nicholas I in his campaign against the Raskolniks
and sectarians closed Vyg in 1855, and thereafter its colonies became simple villages and gradually fell into poverty.[4] Arctic Russia lost much through the destruction of Vyg.

The Denisovs and their followers, called Pomortsy, or Shore
Dwellers, because they inhabited the Russian Arctic coast, expressed their doctrine in a symbolic book *The Shore Dwellers'
Answers,* written in 1723 in reply to 106 questions asked by
Father Neophyte, an Orthodox missionary, who visited them in
1722. The *Answers* began with the full profession of the Orthodox faith as it was understood before Nikon. They advocated the
ancient sign of the cross, the double " Alleluia," and the ancient
icons. The *Answers* admitted that the Church might exist without a priesthood, and in that case there could be only two sacra-

ments: baptism and penance. In the absence of the Eucharist the fervent desire to communicate was sufficient.

The Shore Dwellers' doctrine of the internal temple in the soul influenced not only the more radical Priestless groups but also the Dukhobors and other mystical sects. This doctrine is stated very clearly in the *Answers:* " All assemblies and services, feasts, communions and sacrifices were established to purify man of his sins in order that God may come in. The soul, which bears God, does not attach itself to the visible churches and sacrifices, to the numerous congregations and human feasts. It does not worship God on this mountain or in Jerusalem. The soul has God within itself, true spirit, interior altar-pure conscience, non-material purifying tears, interior Jerusalem, joy of the spirit. The soul, being spiritual, brings forth spiritual sacrifices." [5]

The Shore Dwellers' liturgy included all services that could be performed in the Orthodox Church by laymen. For the maintenance of order and piety, the Shore Dwellers elected certain laymen to act as their teachers and ministers. These teachers occupied among them a place not unlike that of the rabbis in post-Biblical Judaism. All the genius of the Denisovs and all the fervor of the Shore Dwellers were, nevertheless, unable to prevent the disruption of the Priestless into a congeries of sects, or *tolki*. Their divisions all were centered around the problems of marriage and relations with the state and society at large.

Assuming that the priesthood and all the sacraments dependent on it, including marriage, disappeared from the world after the time of Nikon, the Priestless prescribed compulsory celibacy as a matter of principle. They advised it too as a matter of expediency as they awaited the speedy end of the world. Demanding lifelong chastity for everybody, the Shore Dwellers separated the married couples once they rebaptized them. The manifest impossibility of practicing universal celibacy forced the Priestless to tolerate concubinage among their followers, and even Vyg itself was not free from that weakness. Such disorder led several eminent monks to abandon the Priestless and return to the Church. Concubinage often led to abortion, child murder, and illegitimacy; and this moral degeneration of the Priestless alarmed their best elements.

A way out of the impasse was sought eagerly, especially after the sect was subjected to an official investigation.

A discontented Vyg monk, Ivan Kruglov, in 1738 reported to St. Petersburg that the Vyg people were proselytizing among the Orthodox and rebaptizing them. Furthermore he reported that they had abandoned the rite of marriage and that they considered all Orthodox patriarchs and bishops and even the empress Anna herself to be unbaptized. For this reason they were refusing to pray for the empress. The next year the Government sent a delegation of clergy and soldiers led by Kvashnin-Samarin to conduct an investigation. The extremist members of the Vyg sect wanted to burn their monasteries and themselves in order to avoid the threat of seduction from their beliefs and practices; but Simeon Denisov, the bolshak, opposed such a radical step. Rather, he agreed to introduce prayers for the empress into the services. This gesture of loyalty to the Government satisfied Kvashnin-Samarin, and he left Vyg without calling for persecution.

The Shore Dwellers survived their early period of radicalism and excess and settled down to become a sect of well-to-do peasants and merchants, who were law-abiding and God-fearing citizens. Instead of being a menace to the Government, they became its supporters, and as time went by they became more and more moderate in their practices. They allowed their members to eat and drink with outsiders and eventually even to marry them. In Moscow, where a merchant, Monin, built a chapel for them, the Shore Dwellers officially accepted marriage and in 1765 were on the point of becoming Priestists. Many of them did eventually turn either into Priestists or Edinovertsy. An official estimate in 1863 numbered the Shore Dwellers at over two million, but their strength declined after that time.

THE THEODOSIANS

After the Shore Dwellers effected a partial reconciliation with the imperial regime, the more radical of the Priestless believers combined into extremist sects. For a time the Theodosians were the most radical of the Priestless groups. Their founder was Theo-

dosius Vasiliev, a lay reader from Vyshnii Volochek. Originally
an inmate of Vyg, he was sent from there to Poland to organize
the Priestless fugitives in that country. Instead of subjecting them
to Vyg, however, Theodosius in 1706 organized his own sect,
which bore his name. He was imprisoned in 1711 at the order of
Job, metropolitan of Novgorod, and soon died in prison.

Theodosius differed from the Denisovs of Vyg primarily on the
issue of celibacy. While the Denisovs imposed compulsory celibacy on everyone, Theodosius considered this rule to be imprac-
ticable and absurd. He did not separate those who were married
in the Russian Church. He admitted, with some inconsistency,
the validity of such marriages for his followers.[6] Denisov on the
other hand, could not see how these marriages could be valid if
the priests who celebrated the wedding ceremonies were not
Christians themselves.

Furthermore, Theodosius and the Denisovs could not agree on
the problem of the proper relationship with the State. When
Simeon Denisov in 1738 introduced prayers for the Russian empress Anna into the Shore Dwellers' services as the only alterna-
tive to save his monastery from State supervision, he justified the
innovation by appealing to the Scriptures — particularly to Paul
who prescribed prayer for the pagan Roman emperor. Such an
accommodating attitude failed to satisfy the Theodosians, who
argued that although praying for a pagan ruler was all right,
praying for Antichrist was an entirely different matter! If the
Russian Church is the synagogue of Antichrist and the Russian
State supports it, the Russian State is necessarily the work of
Antichrist; and to pray for rulers who serve Antichrist is blasphemous, the Theodosians reasoned. Furthermore, the Theodosians
taught that it was equally sinful to observe the law of Antichrist's
state; consequently they prohibited their followers from obeying
the imperial laws and from appearing before the magistrates.
They urged their followers to live as a separate community, reducing intercourse with the heretics to a minimum. It is interesting to observe that two centuries after the time of Denisov and
Theodosius at the time of the beginning of the Soviet regime a
similar problem arose concerning the proper relationship between

the Church and a hostile State. The issue mightily agitated Russian churchmen in the Soviet Union and abroad and brought about a division along familiar lines. The majority, led by Patriarch Sergius I, accepted finally Denisov's accommodating point of view, but a strong minority repeated the Theodosians' arguments and adopted their separatist point of view toward the State. Until now these " neo-Theodosians " dominated the point of view of the Russian clergy and laity living outside of the Soviet State.

As far as marriage was concerned, the Theodosians, in direct defiance of their founder, soon adopted most radical views. The council held by the Theodosians in 1752 excommunicated for long terms all those faithful who dared to have children and disallowed any future marrying. This radical position led to the disruption of the sect. Ten years after the promulgation of the decrees of the council of 1752 a young Theodosian, Ivan Alekseev, wrote a voluminous treatise to defend marriage. He asserted that marriage belongs to the province of the natural law and existed before the written law or revelation. He pointed out that the Early Church recognized monogamic marriages contracted before conversion and did not require remarriage of the converts. According to Alekseev, God himself who endowed the contracting parties with desire to procreate and to multiply is the real celebrant of the marriage, while the priest is just a witness for the community. Anxious to legalize the Theodosian children who were born out of wedlock and suffered many civil disabilities, Alekseev advised his friends to marry in the Russian Church. Although he looked upon the priest as a civil servant, a registrar for the State, he recommended that the celebrant have the ancient rite used if that was at all possible. Many people followed Alekseev, who left the Theodosians and formed a new sect called the Newly Married.

Among the old Theodosians the canons of 1752 against marriage nominally remained in force. Although some of them continued to marry in the Orthodox Church and to baptize their children after a proper term of excommunication, the majority persevered in their concubinage and only a hard core of fanatical devotees practiced uncompromising celibacy. A new convention to settle the marriage problem was held by the Theodosians in 1883, and it endorsed the decrees of 1752 and expelled all those members who possessed families. This action finally split the Theodosians into the "Strict Theodosians" with their center at Moscow and the "General Theodosians" in Riga and Poland, where the sectarians early had established several flourishing communities. The Latvian and Polish Theodosians tolerated marriage in varying degrees; therefore they were not in communion with the Muscovite division. The Moscow group received members of the other division readily enough, however, when they gave up married life. The number of the Theodosians was estimated at about one million in 1863, but their strength probably decreased in the years that followed. As far as it is now known, the Soviet Revolution nearly wiped out the Theodosians, whose chief social base had come to be the Russian *bourgeoisie* and the well-to-do peasants.

THE PHILIPPIANS

Among the smaller radical Priestless groups, the Philippians were the earliest to organize. They were named after their founder, a Vyg monk Philip, who continually opposed the opportunist policy of the Denisov brothers. Philip opposed the introduction of prayers for the empress Anna at Vyg monastery. He argued that the empress was manifestly a servant of Antichrist and that to pray for her was to become a servant of Antichrist and to be damned. The fiery preaching of Philip rallied around him many Vyg monks as well as lay Shore Dwellers. Vyg monastery then became such a place of trouble and disorder that its very existence was threatened, and the Denisovs proceeded to denounce Philip to the civil authorities as a rebel and an enemy of the State. Learning of the approach of a military force coming to arrest him, Philip shut himself and seventy of his elect followers into his remote Arctic monastery and fired it. The police found nothing but charred bones. The next two leaders, Terentius and Matthew, arranged similar burnings; and the Philippians venerated these fanatics as martyrs.[7]

The Philippians were exceedingly exclusive and severe. Even the Theodosians were received only after long novitiates and severe penance. As a matter of fact, the doctrine of the Philippians did not differ substantially from that of the Theodosians, however. They did, nevertheless, reject any arrangements with the civil authorities, whom they looked upon as satanic agents; and they imposed lifelong celibacy on everyone without tolerating any relaxation of the rule. With the elapse of time, however, the Philippians, like other radical groups, became more conventional in their practices; and the majority of them went over either to the Edinovertsy or to more moderate sects. Their active center used to be at Voinovo in eastern Prussia; but the preaching of one of the greatest Orthodox converts from the Priestless, Archimandrite Paul Prussky, persuaded this community to join the Orthodox Church as Edinovertsy. Voinovo now is in the Polish Orthodox Church, and the Philippian sect is today practically extinct.

THE WANDERERS

The Philippian sect was radical yet it was not radical enough to satisfy the extremists of the old faith. A soldier named Euphemius, a member of the sect, found the Philippians too worldly for his taste. He had visited Vyg and even became a monk with the Theodosians at Preobrazhenskoe, their center in Moscow founded in 1771 by the celebrated merchant prince E. Kovylin, greatest leader of the sect. Nowhere, however, was he satisfied. It seemed to him that all the Priestless compromised with the devil living in the world and that they had become worshipers of the golden calf and prisoners of Antichrist. After lengthy meditation Euphemius started to preach his own doctrine in Sopelki, in the province of Yaroslavl, where a good many of the people were itinerant merchants and peddlers.

Euphemius proclaimed boldly that the imperial power was the apocalyptic beast and that the civil authorities were images of the beast while the clergy were its body. It is foolish to live among the satanists, as the Priestless do, and to pretend to be saved, he said. No one can be saved in the satanic society; rather, the only way of salvation, he taught, is to leave this corrupt world and to hide in remote places. Since a true Christian must avoid any intercourse with the damned, Euphemius forbade his followers to take any certificate of identity, to pay taxes, or to become soldiers. He who wants to be a Christian or Strannik (Wanderer) must die to the world, baptizing himself in a river by triple immersion. He then must become a pilgrim traveling from place to place, avoiding any contact with state agents, who are servants of Antichrist.[8]

The followers of Euphemius, who were called the Wanderers, developed slowly and never became numerous. They established their center in Sopelki, where Euphemius died in the 1780's. Like the medieval Cathari, they were divided into two groups, those who go from place to place and those who remain at home. The "home Christians" usually were well-to-do peasants who acted as hosts to the Wanderers on the road, but they vowed to take to the road before they died. Only when they actually started to wander were they rebaptized. The Wanderers' rules were exceedingly severe and strongly recall those of the early Franciscans. No Wanderer could touch money because the image of Antichrist was impressed upon coins. Many thought of the Wanderers' life as full of adventure and romance and were powerfully attracted to the movement.

Highly individualistic, recognizing no authority whatsoever, perfect anarchists in fact, the Wanderers occasionally fell into grievous sins of the flesh and even committed crimes. Then they purified their lapses with most extraordinary penances. It seems that the well-known Gregory Rasputin knew intimately this sect and even lived as a Wanderer for a time. Impressed by the absence of any control over the Wanderers, one of their leaders, Nicetas Semenov, decided to organize them. He drew up eighty-four articles for their observance which set forth a system of government and supervision. Many Wanderers rebelled against Semenov's legislation, but the majority adopted it. The Wanderers were first composed of fugitive serfs, deserters, and all those who hated the imperial regime, nobility, *bourgeoisie,* Established

Church, and ecclesiastical organization of any kind. Later they became more sedentary, and finally most of them turned into well-to-do people who never wandered. They did try to die in their gardens, however, so that they could say they had left home.

A minority, nevertheless, continued to practice vagrancy, and for them special houses were established where they rested for long periods and meditated. Children also were brought to these houses as future Wanderers. Those who wanted to become Wanderers were admitted first as novices, and their novitiate lasted three years. After a successful novitiate the candidates became home Christians. In this estate they continued to live in the world and to keep their shops and businesses, but they received the true Wanderers into their homes and kept the Wanderers' houses of rest and schools for children. Most of the Wanderers remained at that degree for life and became true Wanderers only on their deathbeds. Only the more adventurous progressed farther and became catechumens. Finally they were admitted to rebaptism, losing everything to become Pilgrims — Stranniki — having no name, property, money, or passport.[9]

The Saviourites

According to Andreev's *Raskol i ego znachenie v narodnoi russkoi istorii* (page 188), there were 130 different Raskol sects in Russia in 1870. This multiplicity of sects and their continuous subdivisions could not fail to confuse many Raskolniks. As a reaction, the Convention of the Saviour — Spasovo Soglasie — made its appearance. Opposing all the other Priestless groups the Saviourites denied flatly that a layman could baptize or perform any sacrament whatsoever. According to the Saviourites, all sacraments performed by laymen were invalid and blasphemous.

The Saviourites taught that since Antichrist came to rule the world, saving grace is lost. The age of sacraments and public worship has passed forever, and the only way of salvation which God has left to men is in direct union with him through prayer. A Christian must surrender his entire life to the Saviour, who knows how to save him. Accordingly, the Saviourites based their conduct, like the Quakers, on the inner voice and divine inspiration. Yet, unlike the Quakers, they were not fully consistent. In order to escape the reproach that they were not Christians because unbaptized, the Saviourites baptized their children and married themselves in the Russian Church. Admitting that the Orthodox Church was heretical, the Saviourites prayed that God, seeing the simplicity of his people, would transform the empty rites into saving sacraments.[10] The Saviourites forbade strictly the rebaptizing of converts and received them through a simple abjuration of their heresy.

The Raskol broke the unity of the Russian Church. The Priestists, who never wandered far from the Church, either returned to it as the Edinovertsy did or came very near after the creation of their own hierarchy in Bela Krynitsa. Although the social base of the Priestists involved the Russian *bourgeoisie,* well-to-do peasantry, and Cossacks, who were destroyed as classes by the Soviet Revolution, the Priestists survived the storm with their organization intact and with an estimated three million faithful.[11]

The history of the Priestless was different. With every decade they wandered farther and farther from their native ground, becoming continually more extreme and radical. They gave up one thing after another until nothing was left, and they slipped either into religious indifferentism or into the new Marxian religion. First reducing the number of sacraments to two, the Priestless altogether abolished them in the most advanced Saviourite groups. Giving up the ancient, episcopally ordained ministry, several sects abolished all the ministry in due course. Beginning with the most meticulous ritual observances, the advanced Priestless sects dropped afterward everything except private prayers. Starting as the Josephites with utmost support of the imperial power, the Priestless ended in anarchism. Similarly, beginning as the most rigid fundamentalists, the advanced Priestless ended in sole reliance upon divine inspiration.

The Soviet Revolution dealt a shattering blow to the Priestless. The multiplicity of the sects, their doctrinal weakness, and the absence of a strong organization paved the way to ruin. Their advanced elements melted into the Soviet society while their conservatives went over to the Priestists or to the Orthodox. They were three million strong in 1859 and probably numbered eight million twenty years later, but then their rapid decline began.[12] The wealthy Theodosians in Moscow began to enter the Russian Church, and others joined Edinoverie. The Soviet Revolution, it seems, practically finished the Priestless in Russia. Only a few isolated congregations, as far as we know, have remained in the old union. In Estonia, Latvia, Lithuania, and Poland, on the other hand, they survived better. Even there, however, they were unable to resist the ravages of time. Now with the incorporation into the Soviet Union of all their colonies their presumable future will be the same as that of the Soviet Priestless — slow disappearance. They no longer have either ideological or social *raison d'être*.[13]

VII.

PEOPLE OF GOD

The Khlysty

Russian mystical thought, which made its first appearance in the fifteenth century in Saint Nilus' writings, reached its peak in the Orthodox Church four hundred years later in treatises of the bishop Theophanes the Recluse. Russian mystical thought was not confined, however, to the Orthodox Church. It developed also in a peculiar unorthodox way in several small, radical sects usually called mystical sects. The Khlysty, who called themselves " People of God," were the earliest of these sects. Sectarians were discovered in the reign of the empress Anna (1730–1740) and were denounced by the former robber Simeon Karaulov, who reported that the heretics met secretly in four Moscow houses, usually by night. Karaulov's report was investigated, and seventy-eight persons were arrested. The investigators found that the heretics met secretly for their services, during which they danced and jumped, prophesied, and shared Communion bread and water. The sectarians rejected baptism by water, admitting only that by the Spirit. They also rejected marriage although they tolerated extramarital relations.[1] A special court sentenced seventy-eight sectarians to various punishments, and among the prisoners were three monks who were executed.

When the People of God were discovered they already were formed into a well-knit society of some antiquity. According to the Khlysty their sect was founded by a certain peasant from Kostroma province, Daniel Filippov, who proclaimed himself God Sabaoth on Gorodno hill near Murom, in the province of Vladimir in 1631.[2] Throwing into the Volga all the sacred books which he possessed, Filippov declared them useless and their effectiveness abolished. He was himself "God," who had come to give twelve new commandments to mankind.

The followers of Filippov prescribed that he be confessed as God, the Saviour of mankind predicted by the prophets, and forbade anyone to seek any other religion. Sexual relations and the use of strong drinks were proscribed, together with stealing and swearing; and the utmost secrecy about the tenets of the sect and its rites was enjoined. The faithful were to trust unreservedly in the divine voice, which speaks in their hearts.

A masterful personality, Filippov found several people ready to admit his claims. Among his numerous converts he selected a Vladimir peasant, Ivan Suslov, to act as his chief prophet. Thereupon Filippov named him "Christ," the incarnation of the Son of God, and sent him out to preach his doctrine. Suslov, in his turn, appointed twelve apostles to assist him and found a woman ready to act the part of Our Lady. Suslov preached the new religion with great success on the Upper Volga, where great crowds flocked to him, rendering divine honors. The preaching of Filippov and Suslov soon attracted the attention of the Moscow Government, and both heresiarchs were arrested but soon freed as harmless madmen. In 1700 Filippov died; and Suslov died sixteen years later, being one hundred years old.

Procopius Lupin, a Moscow soldier released from service on account of his epilepsy, succeeded Suslov as "Christ." He proclaimed Aquilina, his wife, "mother of God" and became a fervent propagandist of the heresy. He was arrested in 1717 in Uglich; but after being released the next year he went to Moscow. There he recruited many converts, mostly in monasteries and convents but also among layfolk. Lupin died in 1732; and in 1733 the sectarians were found out and, apparently, dispersed. Three leaders, nun Anastasiya and monks Philaret and Tikhon, were executed. The corpses of the first two Khlysty "Christs," Ivan Suslov and Procopius Lupin, buried in Ivanovsky monastery, were disinterred and burned in 1739.

As was the case with earlier Russian secret sects, the Strigolniks and the Judaizers, the Khlysty did not disappear but merely "went underground." In the very year when the bodies of the heresiarchs were burned, the sect began to spread widely once more. People of God found a new "Christ" in the person of a peasant, Andrew Petrov, who was a shrewd and able propagandist. Several great nobles were impressed by him, and some joined the sectarians.[3]

New proceedings against the Khlysty began in Moscow in 1745. In a series of investigations and trials that lasted for seven years, 416 persons, including priests, monks, nuns, and layfolk, were implicated. The court sentenced several heretics to penal servitude or to imprisonment, but those who recanted were pardoned. This severe treatment, however, did not stamp out the Khlysty movement. Another "Christ" appeared in Tambov province near the beginning of the nineteenth century who believed that he saw God face to face and received a mission to convert mankind. His name was Avvakum Kopylov, and he was a silent, retiring peasant, a widower. He found a few followers among the neighboring peasants, nevertheless, and selected a certain Tatiana Chernosvitova as his "mother of God." For twenty years he spread his teachings until he was betrayed and arrested. He died in prison, while his female companion was deported.[4] Kopylov rejected the Khlysty view that book learning is useless, and he introduced among his followers the rites of penance and baptism.

After Kopylov's death, his son Philip continued his activities; but he soon was eclipsed by another peasant, Perphilius Kutasonov, who established a sect called the New Israel. V. Bonch-Bruevich, the great scholar of Russian sectarian history, believes that the New Israel movement was not only the conceptual but also the *direct* descendant of the heresies of the fourteenth, fifteenth, and sixteenth centuries, such as those of the Strigolniks and the Judaizers.[5] After the death of Kutasonov, Basil Lubkov became the "Christ" of the New Israel. At this time the sect had its own symbolical book, the Catechism, which is very similar to that of the Dukhobors.

An even more radical sect of the Khlysty was that known as Old Israel, which was dominated for a long time by the "Christ" Alexis Stchetinin. Stchetinin was the son of a poor peasant who had settled in the north Caucasus.[6] He was a devout young man; but after some painful experiences, he was converted to the People of God. Thereupon he founded his own sect — Novyi Vek, New Age. A peculiarity of his teaching was that sin is needed for salvation. He held that a man must be immersed in the sea of sin but not drowned there. The destruction of everything dear and holy to man, every attachment, and the equalization of everyone in sin was the chief aim and practical result of Stchetinin's tendencies. He believed that the more a man sinned, the more he suffered, and the greater would be his salvation and future happiness. In his preaching of the necessity of sin, he rejected the sacred character of marriage, parenthood, and friendship and practiced himself all kinds of immoralities and advised others to do the same.

Stchetinin was forced to leave the Caucasus because of his manner of life, and he moved to St. Petersburg. There he joined the important Khlysty congregation at Okhta and sought without success to gain control over it. After the Okhta congregation was dispersed for alleged immoral practices in 1910, Stchetinin, already deposed by his St. Petersburg followers, was prosecuted for all kinds of crimes. In spite of powerful political influences, he was exposed and sentenced in 1915 to civil degradation and deportation. It is interesting to note that Gregory Rasputin, mysterious and influential figure behind the throne during the last years of the Russian empire, knew Stchetinin and apparently practiced his teachings.[7]

The latest known Khlysty sect developed in St. Petersburg near the beginning of the twentieth century. Here some people began to teach that the celebrated Russian priest, a true Russian *curé d'arts,* Father John of Kronshtadt (1829–1908), was a "Christ." A cult was developed around the belief that Father John was a holy man and miracle worker, and the group began to bear the popular name "Ioannity." Although this sect strenuously opposed the Bolsheviks, they did survive the Soviet Revolution.[8]

The Khlysty never were a large group numerically in comparison with the Orthodox Church. Yuzov estimated them to have about 65,000 members in 1880, and they decreased after that time.

Most of the older groups moderated their beliefs and practices in time; the authority of the Bible came more and more to be accepted, and marriage became recognized. Many went over into more moderate sects, and the present-day descendants of the Khlysty are now known as the Pentecostal Christians.

Although the doctrinal positions of the several sects in the People of God varied somewhat, they held in general a common body of belief. The Khlysty pictured the Holy Trinity not as three persons in one Godhead but as three powers or modes of the divine manifestation in man and in the world. Accordingly, they held that Jesus Christ was not truly God but that God only inhabited Jesus by his spirit. Born naturally, just as all other men are born, Jesus was the Son of God only in a figurative sense; furthermore, he died a natural death, and his body was buried at Jerusalem. The attitude of the People of God toward the Bible was that it should be understood spiritually and allegorically, because otherwise it led to contradictions and nonsense. They taught that to die in Christ simply means to die to sin, and to rise again means to abandon the sinful life.

The doctrine of the Khlysty was at the same time pantheistic and dualistic. They believed that deity is immanent in the world. As for man, Adam did fall in sin; but mankind did not sin in him. Everyone sins by his own accord and everyone can be saved by his own fasts and good works. Through a saintly life everyone can become a son of God, a worthy vessel for God to live in as he did live in Jesus. Deity can be incarnate many times, in many persons, and even simultaneously in various persons. Although Jesus Christ was the first divine incarnation, he was by no means the last; and there have been several other incarnations. Just as Jesus Christ was not a unique incarnation, the Scriptures of the Old and New Testaments were not unique revelations. Although they were good and proper for their age, they now are superseded by more modern divine revelations.[9]

The Khlysty believed that the souls of men are created before their bodies, and that the souls migrate from one body to another after the dissolution of the original body. The spirit is the "light," but the body is evil. Sexual relations, which result in the procreation of new bodies, are essentially evil and must be avoided. Adam lost his purity and his place in paradise immediately after his sexual union with Eve. Everyone who marries commits sin, and children are the incarnation of sin.[10]

The origin of the doctrine of the Khlysty is obscure. While some of its features are very similar to Hindu teaching, particularly of certain Vishnuite sects, other characteristics are common to the Manichaeans and Bogomils. The People of God movement appeared first in the Volga provinces, whose traders and sailors traveled often to the Caspian Sea, Persia, and India, where Hindu beliefs could have been absorbed. On the other hand, the Manichaean writings were known in Russia for many centuries, and the Church made frequent efforts to stop them from spreading. Some Russian scholars think that the Khlysty were a purely Russian growth based on the dualism of Russian pagan religion and wrongly interpreted Christianity. A few scholars believe that the Khlysty reflected in Russia some of the Western mystical sects, such as the Adamites and Quakers, as well as the writings of such mystics as Jakob Böhme, Quirinus Kuhlmann, Madame Guion, and Jung-Stilling. Although the later Russian sectarians undoubtedly were familiar with these mystical writers and movements, the older leaders of the People of God certainly could not have known them.

Among the foreign mystics who had the most far-reaching influence in Russia was Quirinus Kuhlmann (1651–1689). He certainly left many traces on Russian unorthodox mysticism, particularly on the Khlysty. He was a strange and colorful personality and probably mentally unsound. A native of Breslau in Silesia, he was educated at the Universities of Jena and Leipzig, where he was greatly attracted by treatises of Athanasius Kircher and Ramon Lull. In 1679, after studying all the writings of Böhme at Leyden, Kuhlmann published his first book, *Neubegeisterter Böhme*. Kuhlmann affirmed in this treatise that true knowledge or understanding of ultimate reality can never be attained through science but only through religious intuition and mystical experience. He denounced contemporary science and rationalist philosophy and predicted the decadence and destruction of the corrupt Christian Churches and sects, the end of the world, and the new Kingdom of Jesus.

Kuhlmann traveled widely in Holland, France, and England, where he published in 1679 *Kuhl Psalter,* which described his visions. In 1689 he came to Russia, where his treatises already were known to the Dutch and German merchants who lived in Moscow. Conrad Nordermann, one of these merchants, became Kuhlmann's disciple. Nordermann went even farther than Kuhlmann in preaching perfect equality among men and communism. Dr. Meincke, the German Lutheran pastor at Moscow, was horrified with Kuhlmann's and Nordermann's teaching and denounced them as heretics to the Moscow Government. The Government appointed two German pastors, Meincke and Vagezir, and two Polish Jesuits, Tichanowski and David, to study Kuhlmann's writings and teachings. All four declared Kuhlmann and Nordermann to be the most dangerous of heretics whose teachings were subversive both to the Church and the State.

Taking no risks and afraid to have new " Judaizers " conducting their activities, the Government condemned both of the heretics to die. On October 4, 1689, they were burned alive. The Russian Orthodox bishops were not consulted in this matter because the two heretics were foreigners and Protestants and were outside of the bishops' jurisdiction. Through Kuhlmann the Russians first became acquainted with Böhme, whose writings greatly influenced not only several Russian sectarians and the Freemasons, but also a number of the Orthodox thinkers such as Soloviev, Florensky, Bulgakov, and Berdyaev. Böhme, however, did not influence the official teaching of the Russian Church at all.

The picture of the end of the world and of the new Kingdom of God as held by the People of God was similar to that of Kuhlmann but was cruder. They believed that no one could enter the Kingdom of God except for the Khlysty, who were temples of the Spirit of God and divine incarnations. The illumination of man by the Holy Ghost, they believed, was prepared by prayer, fasts, and sexual abstinence. Once man became illuminated by God, he needed no guide; God himself spoke to him. Indeed God lived in him and made him a miracle worker. God dwells in man and is incarnated in him. The Khlysty denied, however, any possibility of a union of two natures within man. God only inhabits the body; he never is united with it. The body is essentially vile and corrupt. The People of God believed that they shed these ignoble bodies after their death and became angels of God. Sinners, on the other hand, migrated after their death either into other human or animal bodies or became devils.

Like certain other organizations, the People of God were divided into three "degrees," and members of the lower degrees were allowed to attend only certain services and meetings. The Khlysty meetings usually were held at a meetinghouse with all windows and doors shut. The services consisted of reading the Bible and the Fathers, sermons, and singing of hymns. When outsiders were present, the services progressed in a devout and puritanical way and were hardly distinguishable from the usual Protestant services. The preachers stressed the vanity of life and the pressing need for true conversion. The meeting room was left unadorned except for a few allegorical pictures on the walls. The Khlysty were congregationalist in polity, and each local group was entirely independent. Each congregation was called the "ship" and its ruler the "pilot" or "God," "Christ," or "prophet." The pilot was assisted by a woman minister called either the "prophetess" or "mother of God." The principal officers were assisted by several minor officials, but it was the pilot who ruled the congregation. The prophetess presided at the secret services which were open only to the initiated.

These secret services, the mysteries or "radeniia," took place several times a year, always during the night; and all sectarians, both men and women, took part in them. They assembled in a brilliantly lighted meeting hall, dressed in long white shirts and having lighted candles in their hands. After the usual reading and singing, the sectarians began ritual dances, which included jumping, running, and whirling after the fashion of Moslem dervishes or "holy rollers." Some of the songs sung during these dances suggest the ancient bacchanalian hymns. An extreme nervous excitement, akin to mass hysteria, follows the dancing. At this stage the People of God utter unintelligible words, prophesy, and finally fall down to the ground in sheer exhaustion.[11] Then the lights go out.

Although it has been supposed that the Khlysty fell into orgies of sexual promiscuity, it has not been possible to prove this supposition. Most scholars of the Russian sects believe that such excesses did occasionally take place. Children born of such irregular union were considered, then, to be children of the Spirit, who might become future pilots and prophetesses. The Khlysty had certain rites which can be compared with the sacraments of more orthodox Christian groups. These rites included the ceremony of reception into the sect, the confession to the pilot, and the ritual meal. Outwardly the People of God remained devout members of the Orthodox Church, and they attended its services regularly. They looked upon the Church, however, as a novitiate to the sect, alleging that the Church services and rites were symbols of the sectarian mysteries. They professed the Church rites to be useful for the beginners and harmless to the initiated.

Essentially, the Khlysty were an extreme reaction against the rigid ritualism of the Russian Church before Nikon. While the Josephites proclaimed that all ecclesiastical literature, including pious legends, is inspired by the Holy Ghost, the People of God taught that all the books received by the Church, including the Bible, are human and fallible. To the rigid observance of the most insignificant rites, the Khlysty opposed perfect ritual liberty in their services. Every congregation and pilot legislated for themselves. While the Josephites allowed only duly ordained clergy, the Khlysty appointed their own ministers. While the Josephites stressed the transcendence of God, the Khlysty made him immanent. The Josephites dwelt on the nothingness and moral corruption of man, who continually needs divine grace. The Khlysty, on the other hand, taught that every man is his own savior and everyone may become "Christ" thanks entirely to his personal efforts. The Josephites, although ascetics par excellence, venerated marriage and parenthood; the Khlysty declared sexual life evil and children to be incarnate sin.

THE SKOPTSY

The Khlysty, while despising and abhorring sexual life, failed, nevertheless, to live in perfect chastity. At least the majority of them could not do so. Abolishing marriage, they fell like the Theodosians into immorality and casual sexual relations. Such a fall, such a flagrant contradiction of the People of God's own teaching, could not be allowed to pass unnoticed. A strong reaction was bound to come. New means to overcome lust had to be devised, and a new solution of the difficult problem had to be suggested. The new solution, suggested by Conrad Selivanov, a Khlyst from Orel province, astonished and horrified the world by its radicalism.[12]

Greatly scandalized by the glaring contradiction between the Khlysty's doctrine and their immoral life, Selivanov decided to effect a reformation. Distrusting man's capacity to live chastely by an effort of will only, Selivanov prescribed castration to anyone who wanted to overcome the lust of the flesh. In this way he followed the great Origen. Castrating himself, Selivanov began his propaganda among the Khlysty. Soon Selivanov's friend, Martin Rodionov, joined him and together they succeeded in converting Aquilina Ivanov, the prophetess of an Orel congregation. Yet not until Selivanov succeeded in converting the Tula peasant Alexander Shilov, a first-class propagandist, did the sect begin to grow.

After Shilov's conversion it quickly developed and soon attracted the attention of the imperial Government. In 1772, Catherine II ordered Colonel Volkov to investigate the matter and to punish those who castrate soldiers and peasants. In 1775, Selivanov was found out and arrested. After a severe flogging he was sent to penal servitude for life to Siberia. Selivanov spent twenty years in Siberia. A shrewd and attractive man, he began to pose for Peter III (1761–1762), deposed and murdered husband of the empress Catherine, dear to all the Russian sectarians.

Selivanov alleged that he was the unlucky emperor who had succeeded in escaping the murderers and now was dedicating his life to the salvation of his soul. Paul I (1796–1801), son of the assassinated Peter III and Catherine II, was greatly interested in Selivanov's allegations and ordered him to be brought to St. Petersburg. After a long interview with Selivanov, the emperor came to the conclusion that his alleged father was a lunatic. Accordingly, he ordered him to be put in Obukhovskoy madhouse. In 1802, Alexander I freed Selivanov and personally visited him. The young emperor was charmed and greatly impressed by a gentle and wise old man, and he lodged him at the aristocratic and comfortable almshouse of Smolny.

Selivanov remained at Smolny only a few months. His Polish convert, Alexis Elenski, a chamberlain of the last Polish king, Stanislaw Augustus Poniatowski, succeeded in obtaining the emperor's leave for Selivanov to reside anywhere he pleased. Once free, Selivanov settled in the magnificent house of the merchant family Nenastiev and began his propaganda in earnest. Crowds of people anxious to meet the sage and healer visited him. Services of the usual Khlysty type were held at his house, and they were attended by more than three hundred persons. Selivanov's followers, known as Skoptsy, or Castrates, called themselves either People of God or White Doves (Belye Golubi).

The Skoptsy openly paid divine honors to Selivanov. St. Petersburg society admired him, and the emperor himself visited the heresiarch and asked his advice. Encouraged by this general respect and sympathy, Selivanov restarted his program of mass castration. In 1804 he even sent Elenski to Alexander I with memoranda in which he advised how Russia should be reformed to suit the sect. To the memoranda *Izvestie,* or the Creed of the Skoptsy, was attached.[13] For his insolence Elenski was sent to the notorious Spaso-Evfimiev monastery in Suzdal where prominent schismatics and heretics had been imprisoned since the seventeenth century. Selivanov, nevertheless, was left in peace until 1820, when he was sent to the same monastery for the persistent castration of young men. Selivanov died, reconciled with the Church, in 1832, being one hundred years old.

In the reign of Nicholas I (1825–1855) the Skoptsy were severely persecuted. Yet they were estimated, together with the Khlysty, to be as many as 110,000 in 1859.[14] They spread all over

Russia, mostly in towns among artisans and merchants. Like the Khlysty they soon became wealthy and employed their great capital to foster the sect. The emancipation of peasants in 1861 reduced unrest and lessened their eagerness to join messianic sects. From Russia many Skoptsy fled to Rumania where they founded flourishing colonies at Bucharest, Galatz, and Jassy.

Except in one point, the need of castration for anyone wishing for eternal salvation, the doctrines of the Skoptsy and Khlysty were practically the same. According to the Skoptsy the first man and woman ignored sex. When they discovered it and formed the marital union they fell into sin, and their lust corrupted mankind. Castration is the only means to escape the lust of the flesh and total corruption. Castration was generally understood to involve physical mutilation although some groups of the Skoptsy interpreted it merely as a perpetual sexual abstinence. The Skoptsy taught that all the saints and just men of the Old Testament ended their lives as Skoptsy. Jesus himself was castrated by John the Baptist. In his turn Jesus castrated all his apostles, except Judas, who betrayed him.

The Skoptsy, like the Khlysty, denied that Jesus suffered on the cross and affirmed that he died naturally. His soul ascended to God but his body disintegrated as any other. The apostles and the Early Church practiced wholesale castration; but this great mystery was neglected after Constantine the Great, when a multitude of lustful and unconverted pagans invaded the Church. The Skoptsy believed that Selivanov was the incarnation of God the Son. Miraculously born of the empress Elizabeth, he reigned in Russia as Peter III. He will come again to judge the world. The ritual of the Skoptsy did not differ much from that of the Khlysty, except that they had the so-called baptism by fire, the castration, which was used for men and women alike. The sectarians were divided according to the degree of mutilation into two groups. Under Selivanov the Skoptsy refrained from affirming the periodical incarnation of God among men; but under his successor, Lisin, they gradually reverted to the usual Khlysty teaching. Selivanov influenced many persons in high Russian society during the reign of Alexander I, who was a mystic by nature and became more so after he became emperor. He was implicated in the assassination of his father, Paul I, and suffered all his life with torments of conscience. He hoped to find peace in mystical doctrines which promised to their adepts release from their torments and utter serenity of mind.

THE SPIRITUAL UNION

In Alexander I's reign the most extraordinary societies and sects flourished in Russia. One of them was the celebrated Spiritual Union, founded by Catherine Tatarinov, a society lady, who was associated with Selivanov; and it left many traces on Russian religious and secular history. A Baltic German and Lutheran, Catherine Buxhöwden married a Russian officer, whom she accompanied during the Napoleonic Wars. Unable to live in peace, the couple separated; and soon afterward, the only child of Mrs. Tatarinov died. The distressed lady tried to find her consolation in religion; and she turned to German Lutheranism, which in her age was somewhat similar to Hanoverian Anglicanism, but was unsatisfied. Being acquainted with the wealthy merchant family of Nenastiev, at whose house Selivanov kept his residence for a while, Mrs. Tatarinov began to attend the Khlysty and Skoptsy meetings.

Although she liked the people and their services, particularly the dancing and prophesying, she abhorred the excessive puritanism of their doctrine. She considered the proscription of sexual union wrong and foolish, and she thought the prohibitions on drinking wines and smoking tobacco were unnecessary. The reading of German Pietist authors led Mrs. Tatarinov to a conversion experience, and she joined the Orthodox Church.

In 1817, Mrs. Tatarinov began to organize prayer meetings at her own house. She and her guests read the Bible and commented on it and sang hymns. The meetings quickly became popular and were well attended; and her regular visitors included the powerful prince A. Golitsyn, Imperial Minister of Cults and Public Education, the governor general of the Baltic provinces, and other political, cultural, and religious leaders of the day.

The Khlysty and Freemasons soon began to influence her meetings, and Masonic symbols and songs as well as Khlysty dancing were introduced. So long as the emperor was benevolent and Prince Golitsyn protected the Spiritual Union, it flourished. In 1825, when Prince Golitsyn was dismissed, the Union began to decline and to lose its influential supporters. Nicholas I, who disliked all sects, considered Mrs. Tatarinov to be a heretic and a dangerous person and interned her in 1837 in Kashin convent. In the convent, Mrs. Tatarinov led the exemplary life of a very best nun. She maintained, nevertheless, her view that prophesying and sacred dancing help toward salvation and that the divine grace flows through these expressions just as through sacraments. In 1847 she was liberated and went to Moscow, where she died in 1856.[15]

Most of the unorthodox Russian religious sects of the Khlysty type did not expand into large membership nor was their influence on Russian life as a whole marked for any great length of time. Their significance, however, extends beyond the satisfaction of the researches of the curious. Besides providing symptoms of a variety of social, cultural, and religious dissatisfactions too involved for treatment here, these sects illustrate how persistent religious convictions have been in spite of official disfavor and persecution. The past history of the sectarians furnishes convincing evidence that nonconformity in religion is apt to continue in Russia.

VIII.

RUSSIAN "PROTESTANT" SECTS

THE DUKHOBORS

The extremism of the Khlysty and the Skoptsy repelled many people who had been attracted to their doctrine of the inner guiding light and the indwelling of God in the human soul. This mystical doctrine continued to spread secretly in Russia throughout the eighteenth century and in due time produced the Dukhobors, or Wrestlers with the Spirit, a sect which appeared in the village of Okhochee in the Ukrainian province of Kharkov. The appearance of the new sect in Okhochee has been explained in various ways. Some attribute its beginnings to the influence of Quakers who lived in the neighborhood, while others attribute it to the efforts of a retired Prussian soldier or to the labors of a Pole who had escaped from Siberia.[1] Possibly the new sect was an outgrowth of a dissident Khlysty group; but it seems clear that the Dukhobors derived their peculiar doctrines from a number of sources, including heterodox Protestantism, Freemasonry, and Khlysty teaching.

Protestantism, which was once professed by many Russians in the Polish dominions, penetrated as early as the sixteenth century into Muscovy as well. At a specially convened *sobor,* which sat in 1553–1554, a certain Matthew Bashkin, was sentenced to imprisonment at Volokolamsk monastery. He was the first Russian Protestant with strong Unitarian leanings. Bashkin taught that Christ is not equal to God the Father. Furthermore, he denied the real presence in the sacrament of the Lord's Supper, and rejected the visible Church, confession to priests, and the cult of the saints. Bashkin and the disciples holding this point of view

97

naturally denied the infallibility of the General Councils and rejected the Church traditions almost altogether. Bashkin and his people also were radical in their attitude toward the Bible; they applied the severest kind of criticism and doubted many of its texts.

Two Lithuanian Protestants, Matthew the Pharmacien and Andrew Khoteev, were Bashkin's teachers. Claiming to be Lutherans, these two Lithuanians in reality professed Unitarian views. Since the imperial Government always was tolerant toward the Lutherans, they assumed this guise in order to live undisturbed at Moscow. Bashkin succeeded in gaining to his views two noted Church leaders, Abbot Arthemius of the Lavra of the Holy Trinity near Moscow and monk Theodosius from Beloe Ozero. Threatened with arrest and imprisonment, both monks fled to Lithuania where Arthemius became a stanch champion of Orthodoxy and Theodosius a Unitarian with strong Judaizing tendencies.

Another Russian who took his views from Protestant friends among the foreign residents of Moscow was Dimitri Tveritinov,[2] a Moscow physician in the reign of Peter the Great. Like Bashkin, he rejected the ecclesiastical tradition, the Orthodox conception of the Church, the veneration of Our Lady and the saints; and he considered useless prayers for the dead, fasts, icons, relics, and monastic vows. Yet, unlike other Protestants, Tveritinov did not think well of the doctrine of salvation by faith alone as taught by Luther and Calvin. He considered both of the great reformers to be in error at this point, and he held that a life of good works is imperative for salvation. In fact his position involved the belief that in the end every man saves himself.

Metropolitan Stephen Yavorsky, Russian primate from 1700–1722, saw in Tveritinov a dangerous heretic and ordered that he be arrested. Tveritinov thereupon fled to St. Petersburg in 1713, hoping to obtain Peter's protection. In this he was successful, for Peter the Great liked Tveritinov's views; and under the emperor's pressure Russian theologians found Tveritinov Orthodox. When he returned to Moscow, however, the primate imprisoned him again. The emperor was enraged and prosecuted the primate for contempt of the civil authority. The whole affair was eventually hushed up, and Tveritinov submitted to Orthodoxy and recanted his errors. His more radical disciples, however, proved to be more obdurate and were executed.

It was this kind of unorthodox Protestant tradition that seems to have had influence on the Dukhobors.

Russian Freemasonry, which developed into both religious and political areas not common to English and American Masonic orders, had its influence on the Dukhobors. Freemasonry came to Russia from England. In 1731 the Russian province was created, and Captain John Philipps was made its Grand Master. Freemasonry rapidly spread and soon included in its membership many Russian aristocrats. Up to 1772 the movement in Russia was modeled on that of England, but after that date the mystical teachings of the German Freemasons began to creep in. All the efforts of the Russian Grand Master, I. P. Elagin, failed to stop the steady progress of the mystical trend, which found its center at Moscow.

Johann Schwarz, a Transylvanian German and a professor at Moscow University, became the chief propagandist for mystical Freemasonry. A Rosicrucian and a mystic, Schwarz believed that science without Christianity is the most dangerous poison. He taught that although human nature became entirely corrupt with the fall of Adam, yet all could attain perfection provided they joined the Rosicrucians, who preserved the mystery of perfection. Schwarz was a pantheist to the extent that he believed that God created the world out of himself and not from nothing. The world was, then, a visible part of God, his emanation.

Schwarz died in 1784, leaving behind a strong Masonic organization in Russia; and Nicholas Novikov (1744-1818) succeeded him as leader of the movement.[3] Novikov was a noble and saintly man, an educator and philanthropist who did much for Russian schools, press, and friendly societies. He was hostile to the Jesuits, who were protected by Catherine II; and he attacked them in his writings. The Jesuits, in return, accused him of heresy; and the empress charged Plato Levshin, metropolitan of Moscow, to investigate his Orthodoxy. While the prelate found Novikov's

Orthodoxy to be above reproach, the empress remained suspicious. In the meantime the French Revolution had broken out, and the French *émigrés* spread rumors in Russia that the Revolution had been promoted by Freemasons. Immediate repressions against the Russian Freemasons followed. In 1792 Novikov was sentenced as a potential revolutionary to a fifteen-year imprisonment in the dreaded Shlisselburg fortress, where the emperor Ivan VI had been murdered and where many Russian revolutionaries afterward perished. In 1796, Paul I freed Novikov, who retired then from public life.

Alexander Labzin (1766–1825) continued to spread Masonic and mystical writings in Russia. He translated several treatises of Carl von Eckartshausen and Jung-Stilling, who wrote much about the inner light and immediate union with God.[4] Labzin's translations fell into the hands of a well-to-do Cossack, Silvanus Kolesnikov, who modified them to fit in with the doctrines of the sect that had started among the villagers of Okhochee. In this way Freemasonry made its contribution to the Dukhobors, the name given to the sectarians in 1785 by the archbishop of Ekaterinoslav, Ambrosius.

The Khlysty impact on the Dukhobors became very evident in the messianic claims of some of their leaders. Between 1755 and 1785 the Dukhobor movement was greatly affected by Hilarion Pobirokhin, a Tambov yeoman who, after the manner of the Khlysty, proclaimed himself "God the Son." He selected twelve angels of death and twelve archangels to minister to him and to preach the new gospel. Pobirokhin's activities attracted the attention of the imperial Government, which deported him to Siberia. Thereafter Sabellius Kapustin, a guard's corporal, succeeded Pobirokhin as leader of the sect. He also followed the Khlysty precedent and set himself up as "Christ." It was Kapustin's belief that Christ at first had been incarnate in the Roman popes but that when the papacy became corrupt he was incarnate in various saints and finally in the Dukhobor leaders. In this succession Kapustin claimed to be "Son of God." Before his time the Dukhobors had believed that God dwells in all men but peculiarly in some of them so that each generation possesses its "Christ," who in this way never leaves the world. After Kapustin declared himself " Christ," however, he insisted that thereafter Christ always would be incarnate in his own family throughout the generations.

Kapustin organized his followers in 1802 in Molochnye Vody in Taurida, where the Government deported them in order to isolate them from the Orthodox. There they set up a perfect commune: one treasury, one herd, and one building for the harvest. Everybody received everything according to his needs. The Dukhobors lived by themselves as the New Israel among the heathen. Hard work and sober living made them well-to-do within a decade, and then the usual difficulties arose concerning the just division of earned wealth. The dissensions attracted the Government's attention and the Dukhobors were asked again to move, except those who declared their intention to become Orthodox. The more world-wise preferred the second solution and received as their reward the lands of those who disagreed.

The zealots went to Transcaucasia and settled near Akhaltsikh in 1841. They numbered about 4,000 at that time. The same process as in Molochnye Vody repeated itself. Again the community became well off, and again troubles arose. Sabellius Kapustin was succeeded in his office as the Dukhobor " Christ " by his son Basil Kalmykov, then by his grandson Hilarion Kalmykov, and, finally, by his great-grandson Peter Kalmykov, who died in 1864. Peter Kalmykov's wife, Glycera, succeeded in the Dukhobor rulership. She died in 1886, and with her death the house of Kapustin came to an end. Glycera had wanted to transfer the Dukhobor leadership to her cousin by marriage, Peter Verigin; but a large party of the Dukhobors opposed this decision. A long struggle between the two parties over the communal property greatly weakened the sect.[5]

Verigin's group after coming into contact with the celebrated Russian novelist and religious thinker Count Leo Tolstoy was much influenced by his views. They adopted uncompromisingly nonresistance to evil, denied the right of the state to levy taxes and to register births and marriages, and, finally, rejected altogether the holding of private property, which had crept in during

the previous decades. Tolstoy's and the Dukhobors' views became very similar. According to them both, Christ was a moral
teacher and no dogmatist. He was divine in his mind, which is
the same as in all men. To live rationally is to live in God, to
live eternally. There is no personal immortality — mankind only
is immortal because the eternal mind dwells within it. Tolstoy's
denial of the state was particularly assimilated by the Dukhobors.[6]

In 1898–1899 the Verigin group decided to migrate to Canada,
hoping to live there untrammeled by any state interference.
Helped by Tolstoy, Aylmer Maude, and the well-known Bolshevik V. Bonch-Bruevich and others, 7,400 Dukhobors migrated to
Canada. Tolstoy contributed nearly half of the expenses. The
Dukhobors settled in western Canada, and Peter Verigin, who
had been deported by the Russian Government to Siberia, was
allowed to rejoin them there. The anarchistic views and practices of the sect have resulted in frequent and prolonged conflicts
between the Dukhobors and the Canadian state, which denied
that any citizen is allowed to disregard rights and duties established by law by pleading conscientious objections. Only with
great difficulty and gradually, the Canadian Dukhobors achieved
some kind of *modus vivendi* with the state.

Peter Verigin, known as Petiushka, the last Dukhobor leader,
died on February 11, 1939. J. F. C. Wright has described in his
book *Slava Bohu* the Canadian adventures of the Dukhobors,
which have been many. According to him, there are in Canada
about 17,000 Dukhobors, who are divided into several groups.
Some follow the old tradition, others have made their compro-
mise with the world, and a third group have become near-Com-
munist. The moderate or Independent Dukhobors may in the
future join the United Church of Canada as a group, for some of
them have already done so. The Saskatchewan Dukhobors —
about half of the 17,000 in Canada — have opposed almost unani-
mously having another Petiushka (leader). "Since the death of
the last Petiushka, the sect here has broken up, and I think that
a very good thing," wrote an Independent Dukhobor.[7]

That the Dukhobors in Canada have experienced a grave crisis there is no doubt. Their anarchism and Communistic tendencies as well as their peculiar observances do not fit into Canadian life. They face the necessity of adjusting themselves to the environment of the New World, and the younger generation has done this surprisingly well. Whether the Dukhobors will preserve their peculiar tenets or will dissolve into Canadian Protestantism is a moot point. Those Dukhobors who remained in Russia survived in a few places and are now affiliated with the Pentecostal Christians.[8]

During the leadership of Kapustin, the second self-proclaimed " Christ" of the sect, the Dukhobors came into contact with a Ukrainian philosopher and mystic, Gregory Skovoroda (1722–1794), who helped them finally to formulate their creed. Skovoroda, a native of Poltava, was educated first at Kiev and then at St. Petersburg, where he sang at the imperial chapel. After a long journey through Poland, Germany, Hungary, and Italy, Skovoroda returned to Russia and worked as a schoolmaster at several schools and acted as tutor in many aristocratic homes. He published a number of profound books, but he was unable to settle down anywhere. His unusual views made him either eccentric or heretic in the eyes of his contemporaries, and headmasters discharged him from schools, and nobles expelled him from their houses. The monks, however, were more kind and allowed him to stay indefinitely at their monasteries. In his wanderings across Russia, Skovoroda met many sectarians, some of whom influenced him greatly.

Skovoroda was a very interesting man, but he was an eclectic rather than an original thinker. He taught that the created world is made of material and spiritual principles. In man these two principles oppose each other; and the utter impossibility of serving two masters obliges everyone who is anxious to live in the Spirit to give up all material comfort. The spiritual life and comfortable living exclude each other. The visible world of change hides the invisible God, although God is mirrored in the physical world and is immanent in it. God is pure Spirit; therefore the study of nature cannot reveal him. The Spirit can be understood by the study of spirit only; and since the divine Spirit permeates the human soul, the divine can be apprehended by the study of the human soul. Consequently, Skovoroda taught, self-knowledge, listening to the inner voice, is the only way to know God and to be united with him.

The Dukhobors formulated their first confession of faith in 1791 and presented it to General Kakhovsky, governor of Ekaterinoslav. According to the Dukhobor belief the only source of their doctrine is the living tradition of the sect. This tradition, holy and incorruptible, is derived from Christ himself, having been handed down from one generation to another. The Dukhobors enshrined the holy tradition in their psalter, which includes extracts from the Bible as well as certain hymns of the Church.[9] To the Bible itself the Dukhobors attach very little importance. They point out that the Evangelists made obvious mistakes and contradict each other. Since the Bible has been hopelessly corrupted by ignorant scribes and translators, it may be understood only with the inner light which comes from God.

Pobirokhin, the first Dukhobor " Christ," openly despised the Bible and considered reading it a waste of time since everyone could listen to the voice of the living God who speaks in the heart. Dukhobor theology tends to be unitarian and pantheistic at the same time. With the Khlysty they reject the Holy Trinity and hold that the Father, the Son, and the Holy Ghost are only three manifestations of the same Deity, which may be likened to light, life, and peace. In the human soul memory is the mirror of the Father, intellect is that of the Son, and the will represents the Holy Ghost.

The Dukhobors believe that the Son of God revealed himself in the Old Testament as Sophia, divine Wisdom, which is incarnate in nature, in revelation, and in the saints. The New Testament introduces the age of the Spirit, which dwells in the human soul as the living gospel, the spirit of wisdom, joy, and consolation. Since this inner and living gospel illuminates each man, the Dukhobors do not admit a personal and transcendental god. For them God lives in the generation of the saints and cannot be separated from them. God is ultimately the totality of the saints.[10]

According to the Dukhobors, Christ was an ordinary mortal,

who was inspired by the word of God. He was the Son of God only in the same sense as any other saint. The Dukhobor view of the character of Christ's suffering is that it was not redemptive but rather that it is an example of how men must suffer for truth. Much in the same way as the Khlysty, the Dukhobors believe that while Christ's body dissolved just as all flesh does, his Spirit continues to live in the sectarians. They profess the pre-existence of souls, which were created before the visible earth and afterward fell with the angels. The fallen spirits were punished for their rebellion by being sent to the earth where they are imprisoned in the flesh and migrate from one body to another. The fallen spirits enter the human bodies when these bodies reach the age of discretion, which is between six and fifteen; and it is at this time that Dukhobor children are initiated in the sectarian psalter.

Denying the hereditary character of Adam's sin, the Dukhobors believe that everyone perishes or is saved entirely by his own works and efforts. The denial of original sin necessarily excludes any need for redemption from the Dukhobor theology. Once the fallen spirits are incarnate in human bodies they do not migrate, but the souls of sinners will be exterminated. The Dukhobors deny the bodily resurrection and maintain that the world will remain forever as it is. They believe in one invisible Church of the elect of God, which transcends all races and religions.[11] The Dukhobors, of course, believe themselves to be a true and visible Church, the core of the invisible Church. The Catholic, Orthodox, and Protestant Churches are, in their view, merely human institutions. Strictly speaking, the Dukhobor believes that he personally is the Church, the temple of the living God.

THE MOLOKANS

Simeon Uklein, a son-in-law of N. Pobirokhin, early Dukhobor leader, became dissatisfied with his father-in-law's contempt for the Bible and his claims to be " Christ " and judge of the universe and left the Dukhobors to form his own sect. Selecting seventy apostles among his peasant disciples, Uklein entered with them in a solemn procession into the city of Tambov, the residence of a bishop and of the governor of Tambov province. Acting with extreme boldness and self-assurance, Uklein began to preach his gospel in the streets of the city. The authorities quickly recovered their balance and arrested Uklein and imprisoned him and his companions. After being thrown into prison, Uklein's disciples returned one after another to the Church; and at last Uklein himself denounced his errors and was reconciled to the Church.

Uklein, however, submitted only superficially; and after he was free again, he began to preach his doctrines again but far more discreetly. He achieved a remarkable success. The mysticism of the Dukhobors and their contempt for the Bible astonished and alarmed the average Russian peasant, however dissatisfied he was with the teaching and practices of the Established Church. The Dukhobors were for these potential sectarians far too radical and too alien to Christianity with their doctrine. Understanding the mentality of the Volga peasants and their love for the Scripture, Uklein reformed his Khlysty-Dukhobor doctrine. He proclaimed that the Bible was for him the sole authority in faith. The Old Testament was for him a guide to Christianity and the New its foundation. Christ, Uklein preached, founded one true Church, which visibly existed until the fourth century when the Fathers and the General Councils diluted the pure word of God with pagan philosophy. Nevertheless, the Church did not disappear but survived in small scattered and persecuted communities of true Christians, among whom Uklein's followers take an honorable place. Uklein rejected altogether the allegorical interpretation of the Scriptures so dear to the Dukhobors, and he commented on the Bible with a view to extracting moral and edifying lessons from it.

Yet even Uklein was unable to overcome the strong unitarian tendency of the Russian sectarians. He considered God the Son and the Holy Ghost inferior to the Father, although of the same substance. Christ, according to Uklein, was clothed with angelic and not human flesh. He used the same peculiar flesh which the archangel Raphael had used previously as related in the Book of Tobit. Admitting the resurrection of the dead, Uklein believed that men will receive new bodies, different from those they now possess. He asserted too that the Last Judgment will concern sinners only. The true Christians go to paradise immediately after death while the unbelievers will be sent to eternal punishment.

The social doctrine of Uklein was one of the equality of men. There must be neither rich nor poor, neither noble nor simple, neither masters nor servants. Uklein categorically rejected war and military service and approved those who deserted. The true Christians may obey the secular law but only when it does not contradict divine law. The first of Uklein's settlements on the Lower Volga were founded on Communist principles, and the modern Soviet Kolkhoses [12] are very reminiscent of these communities.

Like most of the Russian sectarians, Uklein was a strong antiritualist and denied any need of sacraments and rites. To justify this position Uklein was forced to resort to the allegorical interpretation of the Bible, which he himself so condemned. So far as rites are concerned, Uklein taught, everything must be understood spiritually. Baptism means hearing the word of God and living accordingly, confession is repentance from sin, and the anointing of the sick signifies prayer. *The Ritual,* or symbolic book of Uklein, states the principal points of his creed and is copiously illustrated with quotations from the Bible. Uklein's liturgy consists of reading from the Bible, commenting on it, and singing hymns. The Orthodox called Uklein's disciples the Molokans, or Milk Drinkers, because they, rejecting fasts, drink milk during Lent, when it is forbidden in the Orthodox Church.

While Uklein abolished Christian fasts he introduced among his followers the observance of the Mosaic dietary law on the advice of Simeon Dalmatov, a convert minister of the Judaizers. The Judaizers, it may be said, never disappeared in Russia. Crushed in the beginning of the sixteenth century, they reappeared several decades later with Theodosius the Squint, then again in the seventeenth century during the Time of Troubles and before the Raskol. In the eighteenth century they spread still farther. In 1738, their leader, a naval captain Voznitsyn, was burned alive in Smolensk together with a Jew, Baruch, who converted him. In 1796, six villages of Voronezh province professed

Judaism, preached by the Jews.[13] Thence the Judaizers spread to all the neighboring provinces, to Moscow and to Siberia, and their deportation to the Caucasus spread their heresy in that region as well.

Dalmatov's Judaistic trend much impressed a Molokan peasant of Saratov province, Sundukov, who began to preach that Judaism is above Christianity. Christ, according to Sundukov, was an ordinary Jew, altogether inferior to Moses, who himself scrupulously observed the law. Therefore, Sundukov argued, it is altogether preposterous and harmful to observe any feasts and rites other than Jewish. Sundukov's disciples went still farther. They united with the old sect of the Subbotniks, survivors of the Judaizers, who numbered in the 1880's 3,173 people according to the Government's estimates, but probably were far more numerous. Although rigorous repressions of Nicholas I, who settled the Subbotniks in the Caucasus, slowed down their growth, they continued to develop.[14]

"The Caucasian Subbotniks are, according to *The Jewish Encyclopedia,* probably descendants of the Khazars. Their type is more Slavonic than Semitic but their mode of life is Jewish; they not only keep the Sabbath strictly, but also observe all the Mosaic Laws and many rabbinical precepts. In Tiflis in 1894, their community numbered 30 families, besides many who lived outside the village and occupied themselves with cattle-breeding, agriculture, and cultivation of the vine. They have the same prayers as the Russian Jews but use the Russian language instead of the Hebrew. Some of them send their sons to Wilna for a higher rabbinical education. They consider it a great honor to intermarry with rabbinical Jews." [15]

The still more radical Judaizers, or Gerui (from Hebrew converts), are pure Jews in religion although they are Russians by race. They pray in Hebrew, live according to the rabbinical prescriptions, have Jewish rabbis, and expect in the Messiah the sovereign of the whole world. The Sabbatharian Molokans never went this far. Although they rejected the Holy Trinity, they accepted Jesus as a prophet. With the Jews they await another Messiah, a great lawgiver, who will establish on earth the Kingdom of freedom, justice, and wisdom. The majority of the Molokan

Subbotniks accepted all the Jewish rites, including circumcision. They pray in Russian but use the Jewish prayer book, well translated.

THE COMMUNAL MOLOKANS

The Judaistic tendencies of certain Molokans naturally produced a strong reaction. Those who opposed them were called Voskresniks or Sunday Observers.[16] One of the Voskresniks, Maximus Popov, founded the sect of Communal Molokans. A well-to-do Samara peasant, he gave all his fortune to his followers whom he organized into a commune on the lines suggested in The Acts of the Apostles. In the beginning, the sectarians possessed everything in common but this did not work satisfactorily.

While Popov was at the head of the colony it was the perfect commune, to which utopian Communists always aspire. When he was deported, however, the better-off sectarians abolished his organization and introduced instead a communal fund to which everyone contributed one tenth of his income and, besides, voluntarily, periodical donations. From this fund the needy sectarians could receive loans and grants on certain conditions. The community was administered by the Council of Twelve, which was presided over by the judge, whose duty was to interpret the Holy Scripture. Deprived of Popov's leadership the commune disappeared within a few years. The more clever sectarians dispossessed their weaker brethren.

Alone among all the Russian sects the Communal Molokans reject the principle of private judgment and the unrestrained interpretation of Holy Scripture. Observing to what extent private judgment pulverized the Russian sects as well as Western Protestantism, the Communal Molokans vested the interpretation of the Bible in one single man, whom they elected. Anyone who dared to comment on the Bible in any other way than the judge did was immediately expelled from the sect.

THE JUMPERS

The oligarchical tendencies among the Communal Molokans produced a strong reaction. The democrats, objecting to the es-

tablishment of the Council of Twelve and the judge, left the
sect and started their own society, which soon became known as
the sect of the Jumpers. The Jumpers returned to the old Khlysty ritual of sacred dancing and prophesying. They revived the
Khlysty office of Christ and renamed him czar. The best known
among the Jumpers' czars was a certain Maximus Rudometkin,
who was actually crowned by his followers in 1857 as the King
of the Spiritual Christians.[17] The next year the imperial Government arrested and deported him. Gradually the Jumpers began
to approximate the Subbotniks, preserving, nevertheless, their
own Khlysty features.

The Jumpers are spread mostly in the Caucasus and in the
Ukraine. V. Yasevich-Borodaevskaia attended a Jumpers' night
service in Ekaterinoslav province in the Ukraine and described it.
She was much impressed and horrified. Singing and dancing
were ecstatic and often hysterical. The ritual was more or less
that of the Khlysty. She thinks also that the German Mennonite
sect of the Hüpfer, or Jumpers, which had many followers in
the German colony of Kichkas, influenced the Ukrainian Pry-
guny or Jumpers. The Jumpers' big village, Shirokoe, is close to
Kichkas.[18] The Jumpers were spreading fast in the last years of
the empire. They survived the Bolshevik Revolution and are included now among the Pentecostal Christians.

While the Molokan radicals drifted into Judaism or reverted to
the Khlysty idea, the moderates progressed toward a more orthodox Protestantism. The moderates were headed by Isaiah Krylov,
one of the most intimate disciples of Uklein, a great authority on
the Bible. Krylov pointed out to his coreligionists that they arbitrarily and unlawfully suppressed several rites, mentioned and
ordered in the New Testament, particularly the Lord's Supper.
Accordingly, Krylov introduced among the Molokans several
rites and observances, including kneeling, bowing, and the kiss of
peace. Maslov, Krylov's disciple, further developed the Molokan
ritual. He wrote a proper Communion service with reading from
the Epistles and from the Gospels and the blessing of bread and
wine. He also introduced the churching of women, auricular confession, and the solemnization of marriages.

THE EVANGELICAL CHRISTIANS

Andrew Salamatin, a Don Cossack, introduced Maslov's ritual among the Molokans of southern Russia, founding the so-called Don Connection or *Tolk*. To these Molokans, the name " Evangelical Christians " was gradually granted by all concerned. The Don Molokans are very near to the Anglo-Saxon Free Churchmen in their ways. They are also closer to the Orthodox Church than any other Russian sectarians. They have the churching of women, baptize by the triple immersion, confess sinners with the reading of the prayer of absolution, possess the fixed form for the Lord's Supper, anoint the sick with oil, pray for the Government, serve in the armed forces, and are loyal citizens.[19] They elect and ordain their ministers. All those present lay their hands on the candidates.

The Evangelical Christians are now closely associated with the Baptists but they preserve their peculiar rites and autonomous organization. The Evangelicals after the Baptists are the most important and influential Russian Protestants. They still possess a good many congregations in the Soviet Union as well as abroad, particularly in Manchuria and the United States. They absorbed a good many other Molokans and gained several converts from the Orthodox and unbelievers. It is not possible to state their size since there are no reliable statistics, but one million would be a tolerable guess.

The absence of any definite creed, continuous bickering and struggles among the numerous Molokan factions, failure of the leadership, and sectarian narrow-mindedness nearly finished the Molokans. N. F. Kudinov, a member of the All-Russia Molokan conference in 1905, was pessimistic about the Molokans' future, but they have survived.[20] Russian Protestantism was saved, however, by the Baptists, who have absorbed many Molokans.

A. Plotonov, editor of the Orthodox periodical *Missionerskoe Obozrenie,* has written rightly that " we are on the eve of the widest spread of Baptism which must attract our special attention. Russian Baptism has a fine, strictly controlled organization, large capital, a big publishing business, good preachers and speak-

ers, a large number of the well disciplined and devoted missionaries. Russian Baptism is strong with its moral living. It directs
now its efforts to absorbing dozens of thousands of Molokans —
which is important for us.

"Molokanism and Baptism among the sects are very much
like the Priestists and the Priestless in the Raskol. As there the
Austrians (Priestists) develop more and more on account of the
Priestless so it is between the positive Baptism and the Molokans.
A naïve rationalism is easier to overcome by preaching than a
scientific rationalism or, generally speaking, a culturally developed conscience which it absorbed. Therefore, the struggle with
Molokanism is far easier than with Baptism." [21] These words,
written forty years ago, are still true.

Eschatological Sects

Among other sects, more or less close to the Molokan ideas,
can be mentioned the Fraternity of the Just, founded by an Army
officer, Nicholas Iliin, in the middle of the nineteenth century;
the Enochians, started at the end of the last century by an
Astrakhan peasant, Andrew Cherkasov; and the Malevantsy,
founded by a Kiev Baptist, Conrad Malevannyi.

All these sects were eschatological and expected the coming of
the Messiah. The Fraternity of the Just was Communist in its
outlook and puritanical, unitarian, nonritualist, and anticlerical
in religion. The Enochians, who still flourish in the U.S.S.R.,
await the end of the world. According to them the predicted return to the world of Elijah and Enoch already has taken place.
They came as Fr. John of Kronstadt and Fr. Nicholas Blago-
vestchensky. Nicholas II was Antichrist, who murdered the emperors Alexander II and Alexander III and 30,000 people during
his coronation. He enslaved the Church and oppressed people.[22]
Malevannyi simply predicted the end of the world and the new
Kingdom of justice. All these sects reflected the popular expectation of the great social changes which soon were to take place.

IX.

RUSSIAN EVANGELICAL CHRISTIANITY

The Baptists

Of all the non-Orthodox Christian movements in Russia, the Baptists are the closest to Western Protestantism in doctrine and in practice. The Baptist movement, which has been active for less than a century in Russia, grew in size and importance until it became a major force in Russian Evangelical faith. To-day, in spite of certain handicaps, it is exerting a significant influence in the life of the Russian people and has plans for continued growth and activity.

The Stundists, who first appeared in Kherson province in the Ukraine, provided the main foundation for the Russian Baptists, while the Molokans provided another source. Stundism was a foreign importation to Russia. It was introduced by German settlers who abounded in the Ukraine, where they were settled by the Russian empress Catherine II, a full-blooded German herself. German colonies also were numerous in the Caucasus and on the Lower Volga, where, after the Bolshevik Revolution, they formed the Soviet German Republic. This republic was dissolved in 1941 when the German armies rolled to Stalingrad, and the Volga Germans were deported to central Asia, where they still are.

The majority of the German colonists in Russia belonged to smaller Protestant sects, such as the Mennonites and Nazarenes, which were persecuted in their own country by the Lutherans and the Catholics alike. The German sectarians were guaranteed complete religious freedom in Russia but were warned against proselytizing among the Russians. This warning, however, was often disregarded. Russian Stundism was initiated in 1867 by

Pastor Bonekämpfer, who served the Nazarene community of Rohrbach and indulged in proselytizing propaganda.

Bonekämpfer's propaganda prepared the ground for activities of another German, Martin Hübeer, a blacksmith. Hübeer, a Baptist, succeeded in converting to his creed a Ukrainian peasant of the village of Liubomirka, Ivan Riaboshapka. Knowing full well what to expect for rebaptizing Riaboshapka, Hübeer left to another Russian convert, a peasant named Tsimbal, the performing of the rite. Riaboshapka succeeded soon afterward in converting another peasant, Michael Ratushny, who became the leader of the movement and its gifted propagandist.[1]

The converted peasants stopped going to Orthodox Church services and started to meet together in private houses for their own services, which the German Pietists called "Stunden," or "Hours." For this reason the converted Kherson peasants became known as Stundists. At their meetings the converts read the Russian Bible and asked the German pastors and laymen to comment on it. In due time the authorities noticed Ratushny's association with the German Nazarenes and his prayer meetings, and he was arrested and deported for the formation of an illegal society. His deportation, however, did not stop the movement. Ivan Riaboshapka, Gerasim Balaban, and James Koval continued the work of Ratushny in different Ukrainian provinces.

Another center appeared in the province of Ekaterinoslav, where Johann Neubauer, a German Mennonite, married to a Russian woman, started to convert peasants in 1879. He prepared the ground for another propagandist, Andrew Stoialov, who in 1883 baptized thirteen persons near the Mennonite colony of Friedensfeld. From the Ukraine, Stundism spread to Great Russia, finding its first converts among the dissatisfied Molokans and Khlysty.

The Stundist doctrine was similar to that of Western Protestantism. Accepting the Bible as the only source of their faith, the Stundists rejected the cult of Our Lady and saints, prayers for the dead, and the multiplicity of rites. They prescribed to their adherents a strict rule of life involving abstinence from strong drinks, smoking, and dancing.[2]

Besides in the Ukraine, Russian Baptists, in a different form and against a different background, also appeared in Transcaucasia. Again the German settlers were propagandists. Martin Kalweit, a German artisan from Lithuania, was the pioneer. Kalweit had been a Lutheran from his boyhood, but he became dissatisfied with Lutheranism, which he did not consider radical enough; and in 1858, he joined the Baptists. Four years later Kalweit migrated to Tiflis, capital of Georgia, where he found a flourishing Molokan community with indubitably Judaizing tendencies.[3]

Kalweit became friendly with Nicetas Voronin, a prosperous merchant and the leader of the community, and the two began to discuss religious subjects. These discussions ended with Voronin becoming a Baptist, but he embarrassed Baptism with his great fervor and soon started to proselytize among the Molokans. Gradually a small Baptist community was built up in Tiflis, and in 1870 a very gifted Molokan youth, Basil Pavlov, joined the group. In his reminiscences Pavlov says: " My parents were Molokans. This sect is nearly Protestant but like the Quakers they reject baptism and the Lord's Supper. Reading the New Testament and talking with the Baptists I became convinced that I must be baptized. I joined the Tiflis Baptist community in 1870, being sixteen years old. The group had just come into being and consisted of a few persons. My parents were against my doings." [4]

A fine preacher, Pavlov soon attracted crowds of the Molokans to Baptism. In 1875, the Tiflis congregation sent Pavlov to the Baptist Theological College in Hamburg, where he was ordained in 1876 to the ministry by the celebrated Baptist missionary Oncken. In 1876, Pavlov returned to Russia and began to convert the Jumpers of Vorontsovka, who asserted that they had special gifts of the Holy Ghost, including prophecy and speaking in foreign tongues. The Jumpers observed several Jewish festivals, danced during their services, and organized communal meals called " sacrifices." On his return to Russia, Pavlov met Ratushny and discussed with him Baptist prospects in Russia. In this way both of the Baptist movements in Russia became linked.

Meanwhile, a third Evangelical group appeared in St. Petersburg. A noble Russian lady, Mrs. E. Chertkov, whose son died in 1865, embraced Protestantism during his illness. Visiting afterward in England, Mrs. Chertkov became friendly with Lord Radstock, a Victorian revivalist of the Plymouth Brothers variety. She invited him to come to Russia where many people, she assured him, would like to hear him. Lord Radstock accepted Mrs. Chertkov's invitation and came to Russia. His preaching greatly impressed several society people, and a good number were converted to Protestantism.[5] One of the converts, V. A. Pashkov, a colonel in the Imperial Life Guards, decided to dedicate his vast fortune to Protestant propaganda in Russia. In 1876, with this aim in view Pashkov founded the Society for the Encouragement of Spiritual and Ethical Reading, which published many suitable books and pamphlets. Pashkov used his numerous estates, scattered all over the empire, as centers for his propaganda. He worked also to unite his own disciples with the Ukrainian Stundists, Caucasian Baptists, and Russian Molokans.

In 1884, Colonel Pashkov convened a conference in St. Petersburg which leading Russian and foreign Baptists attended. Pashkov wanted to unify all the Russian Protestants into a single centralized and dynamic movement, but he failed to accomplish this end. The question of baptism presented the greatest difficulty. While to the Baptists proper it was the condition *sine qua non* for being a Christian, to many Molokans it was but an empty and superfluous rite. The conference failed to unite the Russian Protestants, but it did bring upon them severe persecution. In the Russian empire proselytizing among the Orthodox was a punishable offense, involving, according to Article 189 of the Criminal Code, imprisonment up to four years and deportation to Siberia, combined with the deprivation of nearly all civic rights.

So long as the Baptists proselytized among the Molokans, the Government did not care, but once they touched the Orthodox the penal laws became operable. In 1884, the Government dissolved Pashkov's Society and banished him from Russia. He died in Paris in 1902. Serious efforts were made by the authorities to suppress the Russian Baptist movement. The Government, led by an able lawyer, Constantine Pobedonostsev, high procurator to the Holy Synod, became convinced that the imperial regime had been undermined by revolutionary propaganda and could be saved only by the strictest application of Uvarov's formula: Orthodoxy, Autocracy, Nationalism.[6] It was a widely held belief that in order to remain a great power, Russia must preserve intact its unifying spiritual force, the Orthodox Church; its centralized autocratic government and the predominant position of the Great Russians and their language among all others.

From this point of view all religious separatists among the Russians proper were destroyers of their own spiritual and cultural unity and were potential traitors. The Baptists and the Russian Catholics, being closely connected with the West, were most obnoxious to the rulers. Further repressions followed the dissolution of Pashkov's society. The Baptist Kiev leader, Lassotsky, a former Orthodox, was deported for eleven years. Riaboshapka, after being deported, escaped to Bulgaria, where he died in 1900. The Caucasian Baptists, who formed in 1884 the Russian Baptist Union, electing D. Masaev as their first president, suffered the least. Voronin, Kalweit, Masaev, Pavlov, and Levushkin, all were deported for different terms for their proselytizing propaganda. These deportations cleared the way to the appearance of the most striking figure in the Russian Evangelical movement, Ivan Prokhanov.

Of Molokan ancestry but already the son of a Baptist, Ivan Prokhanov came in 1888 to St. Petersburg from the Caucasus to study in the Technological Institute of the emperor Nicholas I. In St. Petersburg, Prokhanov contacted the celebrated Russian Catholic, Vladimir Soloviev, novelist Leskov, and Leo Tolstoy. He frequented Pashkov's disciples in St. Petersburg, who, unlike the crude and narrow-minded lower middle class Caucasian Baptists, were well-educated people with broad views. Prokhanov soon took a leading part in the activities of the St. Petersburg Evangelical community and helped to found the first Russian Baptist periodical, *Beseda*. Although this magazine was quickly suppressed by the imperial Government, its publication continued abroad and much helped the Baptists.

Graduating in 1893, Prokhanov became the director of N. Ne-pliuev's sugar factory but quickly left him, disagreeing in methods. Nepliuev, a wealthy landowner, spent his vast fortune in founding Religious Working Brotherhoods, where the workers possessed factories and estates on Communist principles. After a trip to the Near East, Prokhanov went abroad to study theology and philosophy, first in the Baptist College in Bristol and then in the Universities of Berlin and Paris. Returning to Russia, he worked as an engineer and assistant professor and continued his preaching.

In 1902, he published the well-known Russian Evangelical hymnbook *Gusli*. In 1908, three years after the imperial decree establishing religious toleration was issued, Prokhanov founded the Union of the Evangelical Christians, of which he was first president. Prokhanov did not wish to work in the Russian Baptist Union. He believed that their very name, the Baptists, was alien to Russian people.[7] Besides, Prokhanov was unable to accept the rigid views of the Russian Baptists. In this he was very similar to Vladimir Soloviev, who, although nominally a Roman Catholic, was in reality an independent thinker standing very far from the rank and file of the Roman Catholics. Prokhanov and Soloviev, Russian Protestant and Russian Catholic, were very unlike their Western coreligionists and were in a way heretical.

While the Russian Baptist Union numbered 97,000 baptized members in 1914, Prokhanov's association did not have more than 8,472; but it was rapidly increasing. In 1913, Prokhanov founded in St. Petersburg the first Evangelical Theological College in Russia, which was closed in 1914, however, when the war began. Prokhanov and his friends were suspected by the Government of revolutionary activities and were prosecuted as dangerous men. Their chapels and meetinghouses were closed in large number. In spite of all these difficulties, Prokhanov published the weekly magazine *Morning Star* and calendars, pamphlets, and books of every kind through the Evangelicals' own publishing house, Raduga, which he himself founded. He presided at the All-Russia Evangelical conferences in 1909, 1910, 1911, and in 1911 was elected the vice-president of the World Baptist Alliance.

The fall of the empire was a blessing to the Baptists. The Liberal Provisional Government proclaimed in 1917 complete freedom of conscience. The Baptists were at last free to organize as they wished. The first years of the Soviet Revolution were undoubtedly heydays of Russian Protestantism. All restrictions imposed on its spread by the imperial Government fell to the ground. Russian sects, having no endowments, monasteries, seminaries, elaborate hierarchical organization, or ritual, did not suffer to the same extent as did the Russian Church when the law of separation was passed in 1918. The Evangelicals enjoyed full freedom of propaganda and were, for a time, openly favored by the Government, which was anxious to gain their support and to weaken further the Russian Church.[8] Indeed the Soviet printers published for Prokhanov 175,000 books and pamphlets for his propaganda.

The twelfth All-Union Congress of the Communist Party stated: "We must pay the greatest attention to the sectarians, who under the czarist regime suffered persecutions and some of whom are very active. By assuming a reasonable attitude toward them we must win over their most energetic and cultured elements to serve our purpose. Considering the great number of sectarians, this is a matter of the utmost importance. The problem must be solved according to local conditions."

During the first decade of the Soviet Revolution, when the Russian Church was divided and suffered the aftermath of separation, the Evangelicals, helped from abroad, developed intense propaganda. They absorbed nearly all the Molokans and kindred groups, a number of the Priestless Raskolniks and converted crowds of the nominal or disaffected Orthodox. Prokhanov's Union, which numbered 8,472 members in 1914, exceeded 250,000 eight years later.[9] New efforts were made to achieve the fusion of Prokhanov's Union with the All-Russia Baptist Union, but these efforts again failed.

Although Prokhanov was himself the vice-president of the Baptist World Alliance and his Union adhered to essential Baptist principles, they interpreted these principles differently from the All-Russia Baptist Union presided over by P. Pavlov, son of V. Pavlov, the pioneer. In Prokhanov's Union many old Molokan ideas and Pashkov's freedom of thought continued to live, while Pavlov's group closely followed the foreign Baptists. Although an agreement for amalgamation of the two Unions was signed in 1921, it was never implemented. Beyond the nomination of a joint Relief Committee and a joint School Committee, nothing was done.[10]

Meanwhile, relations between the Bolsheviks and the Evangelicals began to deteriorate. The Evangelicals' strong pacifism, close connection with Western " capitalist " countries, and rapid growth of influence among the workers, particularly among the youth, made the Bolsheviks uneasy and hostile. The opposition of the Russian Nonconformists to the collectivization drive, which greatly harmed them economically, decided the Soviet authorities to act. The Evangelicals had reached by this time 3,219 congregations with at least four million members, and since December 1, 1927, they had possessed their own Theological College in Moscow. The Evangelicals of this period were mostly the well-to-do peasants and Cossacks in the country and small shopkeepers and independent artisans in the towns. All these social groups were scheduled for annihilation by the Bolsheviks.

The decree of April 8, 1929, was specially aimed against the Evangelicals. Religious propaganda became illegal. Only freedom of worship was guaranteed. Article 17 of the new decree prohibited the religious associations from forming mutual-aid, cooperative, and productive societies, rendering material aid to their members, or organizing libraries, reading rooms, Bible classes, and women's and youths' meetings. Article 19 restricted the clergy in their travel. Deprived of financial support from abroad, looked upon as potential agents for foreign interventionists, prohibited from carrying on their propaganda and organizing social action, the Russian Protestants began to decline in numbers and influence, particularly after the mass deportation of the wealthy peasants who were dispossessed by the collectivization of the land. While there were 3,219 congregations in 1928, there remained but 1,000 in 1940.[11]

The change of the Soviet official policy toward religion, which began with the permission of the Russian bishops to elect a patriarch in 1943, was followed in due course by the creation of two state commissions to regulate religious affairs. The first commission, under G. G. Karpov, was appointed to deal with the affairs of the Orthodox Church and the second, under Poliansky, was to deal with all other religious groups. Poliansky's job was to assist religious leaders in obtaining from the state supplies and services which they needed. He also registered congregations, preachers, and new appointments. In his interview with Rev. S. Evans, editor of *Religion and the People* (September, 1946), Poliansky expressed his satisfaction with the Evangelicals' war record, particularly with the work of Pastors Y. Zhidkov, M. Orlov, and A. Karev.

War demands promoted a new *rapprochement* between the two branches of Russian Baptists. The leaders of both groups signed in June, 1942, an appeal to Baptists throughout the world. They claimed to speak for four million of the faithful. M. Orlov, Y. Zhidkov, A. L. Andreev, V. N. Urstein, M. I. Guskov, F. L. Burenkov, and A. Karev signed for the Evangelical Christians while T. A. Goliaev, N. A. Levidanto, M. Goliaev, F. G. Patsotsky, P. Malin, V. G. Yakovchenkov, and F. N. Shein signed for the Baptists.

Two years later, on October 21, 1944, both groups of Russian Baptists formed together the Council of the United Baptists and the Evangelical Christians. The Evangelicals predominated in this Council and supplied its president, Y. Zhidkov. The Council invited the Pentecostals to join them in August, 1945. The Pentecostals or Spiritual Christians, a loose association uniting all kinds of sects from the Jumpers and Rollers to the Dukhobors, Judaizers, and Khlysty, which all claim to be guided by the Spirit of God, accepted the invitation. The Council became in this way something similar to the British Federal Free Church Council. The full name of the enlarged federation is the Council of the United Baptists, Evangelical Christians, and Pentecostal Churches and groups in the U.S.S.R. While its president is an Evangelical its vice-president, Rev. M. Goliaev, is the Baptist. The Evangelicals, Baptists, and Pentecostals sit on the executive board.

In 1946, the Council began to publish its own periodical *Brat-*

skii Vestnik. Slogans, taken from the Bible and printed in each issue, symbolize the fundamental beliefs of the constituent groups of the Council. These slogans are: "Striving together for the faith of the gospel" (Phil. 1:27); "We preach Christ crucified" (I Cor. 1:23); "One Lord, one faith, one baptism" (Eph. 4:5). According to the paper the New Council, unlike its stillborn predecessor of 1921, has no desire to exert any kind of pressure on the freedom of conscience of those who belong to it. In fact, it became an organization like the British Council of Churches or the Federal Council of the Churches of Christ in America. While the Evangelicals and the Russian Baptists hardly differ more than do the General and Particular Baptists of the West, the Pentecostals profess views more or less similar to the Quakers and are very much different from the Baptists.

The Council nominated fifty presbyters to act as trustees for communities throughout the Soviet Union. These presbyters act on behalf of the Council with full power. *Bratskii Vestnik* admits that many old-fashioned believers, brought up in the old sectarian exclusiveness, opposed the new arrangement. Their resistance, according to *Vestnik,* gradually has been overcome. That this is actually the case may well be doubted. According to the communication of Dr. W. O. Lewis, secretary of the Baptist World Alliance, to *The Christian Century,* he could not find out what happened to 700,000 Russian Baptists proper. They numbered at least one million before 1941 while in 1947 the United Baptists numbered but 300,000. Suggestions are made that these Baptists left the Government-sponsored organization and "went underground," objecting to the close relations between the new Council and the atheist Government.[12] To the Orthodox "underground" a Baptist "underground" should be added.

Whatever happened to the opposition to the state-blessed organization, its newly appointed elders visited hundreds of communities all over the Union, including western Ukraine and Baltic provinces. In the course of their tour they revived old contacts with local Baptists and Adventists to the mutual advantage of all. The foreign contacts also were resumed. M. Goliaev, the Baptist vice-president of the Council, attended the Baptist Congress in Stockholm in the summer of 1946, and he also visited Finland. The Council accepted, besides, an invitation to send its delegates to the U.S.A. in 1947.

According to Poliansky all the denominations represented in the Council have among them about 3,000 churches. Poliansky admits, however, that this number is merely speculative because no proper census thus far has been made. In Moscow the Baptists and the Evangelicals have together but one chapel, although a second is soon to be built. The present chapel can accommodate only five hundred. Naturally, it is overcrowded. Rev. S. Evans, who attended a service there on Sunday, July 14, 1946, wrote in *Religion and the People* (August, 1946): " I have never seen anything like it in my life. People were standing five deep in the aisles and on every available inch of floor space. The building was literally packed from wall to wall, and the congregation overflowed through the open doors into the street. About 1,200 people occupied a church built for 500. The service lasted two and a half hours. The scene was powerful."

Dr. Louie D. Newton, American Baptist leader, who conducted services in the same chapel the following Sunday, was similarly impressed. Dr. Newton got the clear impression that Baptist ministers are unhindered in their preaching ministry. According to him they are absolutely free in carrying on all their work in their churches, in their homes, and in their communities and orphanages and hospitals, which they maintain out of their contributions. The ministers have daily Bible meetings in their churches, where they instruct their people, particularly children and youth. If such is the case, there is no doubt that considerable concessions have been granted to the Baptists since 1941.

The French pastor, J. Jousselin, and Penry Jones, who visited Russia in 1946 also contacted the Russian Baptists. Jousselin described his visit to Moscow in the French weekly *La Réforme* (August, 1946). " We had hardly arrived," he wrote, " when we were led into the minister's office. He did not know that we were coming, and while they were looking for him, we began to look around. The first object which struck us was a large volume, which we took for a Bible, but which turned out to be a concordance. Our immediate reaction was to suppose that it came from abroad, but this was not the case, as we found it had been edited at Leningrad in 1928. So this concordance had been compiled in the U.S.S.R. under a regime in which all production is dependent on the state, because it is only the state which can supply paper and printing. Still stranger was the fact that this printing was undertaken at a time which was considered the most violent of the antireligious struggle."

Jousselin stated in the same article that " preaching and administration of sacraments are now the sole preoccupation of the clergy. Article 124 of the Soviet Constitution, while allowing freedom of conscience and worship, authorizes only antireligious propaganda. The latter is fast disappearing The godless museums are closed and no godless periodicals are printed. Although no proselytizing meetings are permitted, discussions on moral law and the gospel are possible. About 15 per cent of city people go to church and about 50 per cent in the countryside. The acute shortage of clergy afflicts all denominations in the Soviet Union. The Baptists hope to re-open their Theological College. Meanwhile, they ordain their pastors from devout laymen."

When Penry Jones, who visited the U.S.S.R. in the beginning of 1946, contacted the Soviet Baptists, he found their Moscow chapel packed and its choir predominantly young. The present Christian position in Russia Mr. Jones summed up as follows: " The churches in the U.S.S.R. are free to worship as they please. There is, however, no right to propagate the faith by public meetings, general publications, or through youth groups. The priest or minister may teach children if asked to do so by a family. The churches are thus confined to maintaining the liturgical tradition. They are cut off from the younger generation, and from making any direct impact on the social order. . . . The young products of the atheistic educational system have enthusiasm and vigor, courage and humility, self-sacrifice and self-discipline, and an overruling sense of purpose."

" In Russia, therefore," Mr. Jones continued, " I saw that a ' this-worldly ' Church was of less use than the Communist party.

To be true to her calling, the Church must preach that salvation from sin is through Christ alone." [13] In the Soviet Union all social services — hospitals, orphanages, almshouses, and charities, as well as general education — were in 1918 taken away from the Church. It was left only to worship God and to convert men solely by its own holiness. The Soviet Baptists, as all other Christians in the Soviet Union, had to adjust their message and activities to the new conditions. Since the last war, however, religious groups have been allowed to maintain certain charities.

The Soviet Baptists expressed their creed in a message to the American Baptists sent by them through Dr. Newton in 1946. This document reveals the aspirations, views, and principles of Soviet Baptism and is worthy to be reproduced in full.

Dear Brothers and Sisters in Christ!

Taking advantage of the visit to our country of our esteemed brother, Dr. Louie Newton, communion with whom has afforded us much joy and spiritual pleasure, the U.S.S.R. Council of Baptist and Evangelical Christians, in the name of all our Russian brothers and sisters, sends you a hearty and brotherly greeting. Dr. Newton has asked us to write you a letter, and it gives us great joy to comply with his request. There is much happiness in the life of our Russian Baptist brotherhood, and we feel it of value to share this happiness with you.

We should first of all note several specific features of our spiritual life and activity with which you, Baptists of the United States of America, may be not familiar, and which may somewhat distinguish our Christianity from yours. There are five such distinctive features of the Christian Baptists of the U.S.S.R.

1. The Principle of Unity

Three large rivers — the Baptists, Evangelical Christians, and Pentecostals, who share the Baptist religious principles of resurrection and baptism — have fused into one mighty river whose beneficent waters now flow all over our vast country. All secondary differences which formerly, before our union, separated these three religious currents, are being smoothed out more and more in mutual understanding and brotherly love which are growing and strengthening, in the friendly harmonious work of the Kingdom of God in our beloved land. We fervently thank the Lord for being able to carry out his sacred desire — " That all may be one " — and we should like to see this wish of his for unity among his children become close and dear to all Christian Churches throughout the world.

2. The Preaching of the Pure Gospel

Our entire Evangelical Baptist brotherhood maintains fundamentalist views. We painstakingly preserve the purity of the Evangelistic and Evangelical teaching. The cross of Calvary, the sin offering of Christ, his precious blood — such is the central theme of our dogmatics and our preaching. We seek to bring to the world the pure image of our Saviour just as he is given to us in the pages of the Gospels. We emphasize the divine nature of Christ. We do not deny a single one of his miracles. We do not remove a single one of his words. The complete Gospel is our doctrine.

3. The Preaching of Sanctification

The spiritual depth, purity, and sanctity of the life of our churches and their members — this is what occupies the first place in our educational work. We do not strive for numbers, although we take joy in the conversion of every sinner. Figures interest us very little and we are not especially concerned with statistics of our members. This is a specific feature of ours, and we do not consider it a bad one. The purity of the Church and the highly Christian life of its members are most important for us. It seems to us that in many countries Christianity suffers with the restless spirit of Martha. We inculcate among our members the spirit of Mary, that is, the spirit of deep, meditative Christianity, which is acquired by her stay at the feet of Christ.

4. The Spirit of Early Christianity

The simplicity of the early days of Christianity is our ideal, and we strive for it in all our life and work. We do not strive for outer gloss and noisy advertising. Most of our blessings we received not in luxurious and costly houses of prayer but in simple rooms of the Jerusalem chamber type. We see how often a departure from the simplicity of the early days of Christianity leads to spiritual death and a Laodicean spirit and that the inner life wanes in spite of the outer gloss and superficial beauty of the ritual. We pray unceasingly that our Russian Evangelical-Baptist churches may not deviate from the simplicity of early Christianity.

5. It is our principle to carry on God's work in our country with our own means.

The observance of this rule has developed in our Russian churches the spirit of selfless physical service. Our brothers and sisters have learned to sacrifice not only everything within their power but even beyond their power. In this respect our churches resemble the Macedonian churches. The generosity of our believers finds expression in large offerings which cover all the needs of the work of God in our country.

Complete Religious Freedom. We have listed all the features characteristic of the spiritual life and activity of our brotherhood, and we have complete religious freedom to carry them out day after day. We deeply respect our Soviet Government which has given us this freedom and protects it from any violation whatever. In our country all churches and religions enjoy equal and complete freedom. Because of this freedom we have a flourishing spiritual life in our churches. There is a great fire that burns in the hearts of our believers. The gospel is preached freely, and thousands of sinners repent and turn to Christ. There is not a single church of ours which does not have its conversions. We have information that during the first half of this summer already thirty thousand newly converted souls were baptized. And an equal number will be baptized during the second half of this summer.

We publish a journal *Bratskii Vestnik* [*Brotherly News*] which carries throughout the Soviet Union the news of our work and the blessings from the Lord. We are publishing the Bible, the New Testament, and books of spiritual songs. We shall continue to publish these until we have satisfied all need for this material.

A School for Preachers. We shall soon open a school to train our preachers. The Orthodox Church has anticipated us in this respect, but we shall soon catch up to it. Just as we do spiritual work, we do charitable work. Regular monthly offerings are made in all our churches for the children of soldiers who died during the war. These offerings provide large funds. Ah, if you but saw the enthusiasm of our Russian believers! How much fire! How much love for Christ and our fellow men, how much self-sacrifice, how much simplicity in Christ!

We are far from proud, but we sincerely wish to light the entire world with the light of Christ, and to be a model of living Christianity and the simplicity of the days of the apostles. Accept this letter of ours as fraternal news of those who love you and pray for you, your brothers and sisters in the belief in Jesus Christ, who are scattered over the boundless expanses of our Soviet Union. In the name of the Union of Baptist and Evangelical Christians.

Presidium of the All-Union Council: Chairman, Y. Zhidkov; Vice-Chairmen, M. Goliaev and M. Orlov; Treasurer, P. Malin; General Secretary, A. Karev.[14]

Like the Soviet Orthodox, the Soviet Baptists are strict traditionalists. They have no use for modernists who want to make Christianity acceptable to unbelievers by stripping it of miracles and compromising the divinity of Christ. All groups of Russian Christianity in the Soviet Union reflect the strict puritanism and fundamentalism of their Josephian forebears tempered with the evangelical simplicity and charity of the Nonpossessors.

The Russian Baptists, like the Orthodox, have their own diaspora. A number of the Baptists of anti-Soviet views who fought in the White Armies in 1918–1924 migrated abroad and settled in Manchuria, China, Germany, France, and even in the Americas. In Harbin, Paris, Nice, and in a few places in the U.S.A. and Canada, they organized more or less flourishing congregations, some of which still exist. Among the Displaced Persons from eastern Europe there are a number of Russian and Ukrainian-speaking Baptists and Evangelicals who are organized in several congregations in Germany and England. They recruit quite a number of converts.

The Baptists form the backbone of Russian Protestantism at the present time because of their clear doctrinal teaching and efficient organization. Formerly based on the well-to-do peasants or kulaks and the lower middle class, they survived the virtual destruction of these classes. Their sturdy independent spirit remains intact, however, as they continue to live in spite of strict Government control. Among all the Russian Nonconformist groups, they are the nearest to American Protestantism.

The latest news concerning the Russian Baptists indicates their steady progress. Baptists and Evangelical congregations numbered about 4,000 at the end of 1947. The number of people on the Church rolls was 400,000 while four million attended services. While previously the congregations accepted newcomers relatively easily, now a long catechumenate is enjoined for those who want to be baptized. Only those who really are converted and promise to lead a truly Christian life are accepted. On account of serious demands from newcomers, the congregations are free from unsuitable and unconverted people who only make trouble.

Each congregation is headed now by a presbyter, who usually serves without pay. Only one third of the presbyters are maintained by the congregations. The remainder earn their living as the apostles did, working in factories or on the land. The vast majority of the presbyters are devout but unlearned men, who try to compensate for their lack of proper education by Christlike life. Women take a great part in the work of congregations. The faithful hire the hall and insure services entirely from their own earnings. There are, however, some well-to-do congregations who possess their own chapels, such as those in Moscow, Leningrad, Kiev, Kuibyshev, Riga, and Tallinn.

The Baptist organization is now quite similar to that of the Orthodox. At the top there is an All-Union Council composed of ten members, five of whom reside in Moscow, three in Kiev, one in Riga, and one in Tallinn. The Council for the Baptists takes the place of the Patriarchal Synod for the Orthodox. The Soviet Union is divided by the Baptists into seventy districts, which correspond to the Orthodox dioceses. Each district is headed by a chief presbyter who supervises the ordinary presbyters who lead the congregations. Some chief presbyters continually travel in their districts. The ages of the presbyters vary from thirty-five to seventy.

All the presbyters are registered with the Soviet authorities, as are other clergy, and work only in their congregations. New congregations are started by special workers sent from Moscow who act as missionaries. No one can preach in any registered congregation unless he is provided with a license from the chief presbyter of the district.[15] As is the case with the Orthodox, many Baptists dislike the close control exercised by the State over their Union through the chief presbyters. Therefore they are only too willing to hear unlicensed preachers, who, it is stated, " sow discord in the congregations." There is no doubt that along with the licensed religious organizations in the Soviet Union there are many " underground " groups.

THE RUSSIAN BIBLE

The spread of Russian Evangelical sects and movements was greatly enhanced by the publication of the complete Russian Bible by the Holy Synod in 1876. At this time the Russian people could at last have the Bible in the vernacular rather than in the half-understood Church Slavonic. Saint Gennadius of Novgorod had edited the first complete Slavonic Bible in Russia in the last

year of the fifteenth century. His Bible included all the canonical
books as well as the Apocrypha. Unfortunately, Gennadius' Bible
was written in a very obscure Slavonic which already in his time
had begun to differ widely from the spoken language.

In 1580–1581, eighty years after Saint Gennadius' Bible was
completed, it was published in the Ukraine by Prince Constantin
Ostrozhsky, who vastly improved the text. The Slavonic Bible
was not printed in Moscow until much later, in 1663. The Moscow edition greatly excelled that of Prince Ostrozhsky. Besides,
it followed the Septuagint's order and not that of the Latin Vulgate, on the pattern of which the first two Russian Bibles were
modeled. Revised by several Greek and Slavonic scholars, the
Slavonic Bible was reprinted in 1751 in Moscow, and in 1756 a
new revised edition made its appearance. Since that time only re-
prints had been available. The Slavonic Bible did not entirely
satisfy the Russian need. The spoken language came to vary seri-
ously from the Slavonic and poorly educated persons failed to
understand it properly. Unpardonable mistakes and outright
heresies frequently followed efforts of simple monks and peasants
to interpret the Scriptures.

The publication of the Bible in vernacular Russian was chiefly
due to the efforts of the British and Foreign Bible Society, which
in 1810 began to operate in Russia.[16] Rev. John Paterson, the
agent of the Society, obtained in 1812, through Prince A. N. Golitsyn, Minister of Cults and Public Education, the imperial decree authorizing the foundation of the Bible Society of Russia.
The evangelization of the Moslems and heathen living in the empire and the promotion of Bible study among the Christians were
declared as the two principal aims of the Society. The Orthodox
and Roman Catholic prelates as well as the Protestant clergy were
invited to join the Society, presided over by Prince Golitsyn himself.

The Bible Society, finding ready support from several provin-
cial governors, published in succession the Bible in Slavonic and
modern Russian, Kalmuck, Buriat (Mongol), Armenian, Finnish, German, Polish, French, Estonian (dialect of Dorpat), Estonian (dialect of Tallinn), Lettish, Persian, Georgian, Samogi-

tian, ancient Greek, Moldavian, Tartar, Turkish, Chuvash, and Karelian. All these translations were supervised by the Christian clergy of many denominations, including the Orthodox and Roman Catholic prelates.

At last it was decided to publish the Russian Bible, and the translation of the original into Russian began in 1816. The Old Testament was taken from the Septuagint, and the translation supervised by several prelates and scholars proceeded slowly. Suddenly it was stopped and the Society itself dissolved. This happened because the Russian Bible Society had become a convenient center for Russian Freemasons, mystics, and sectarians, inspired by Böhme, Swedenborg, Jung-Stilling, and Eckartshausen. These enthusiasts even succeeded in strongly influencing several Russian prelates.

Count Alexis Arakcheev, war minister and favorite of Alexander I, disliked Prince Golitsyn and his mystics, whom he considered heretics corrupting the Church. He acted accordingly. In 1824 Prince Golitsyn was dismissed from his ministry and deprived of the presidency of the Bible Society. Two years later the Society itself was dissolved and its assets handed over to the Holy Synod.

Although the slow printing of the Russian Bible went on, in 1836 it was again stopped by Count Protasov, the high procurator of the Holy Synod (1836–1855).[17] This pupil of the Jesuits looked upon the Slavonic Bible in the same way as the Latins do on the Vulgate. The Slavonic text was for Protasov a sacred inheritance from the ancestors, the common treasure of the Slavs. He considered it quite adequate for the Church services and private reading by educated persons. Protasov considered the Russian Bible not merely useless but positively harmful in a country full of sects and almost illiterate. To distribute the Russian Bible among the illiterate peasants and artisans would accomplish nothing, according to Protasov, but the spreading of sects. The future largely justified Protasov, who, unsatisfied by merely stopping the printing of the Bible, ordered the books already printed to be destroyed.

Only in 1858, after Protasov had retired, did Archpriest Pavsky and Archimandrite Macarius (Glukharev) succeed in securing permission to resume the publication of the Russian Bible. In 1876 the complete Russian Bible was on sale, and the Russian Protestants received their Bible from the Holy Synod. The translation was accurate and clear, and the language refined and solemn. Since then the British Bible Society has reprinted this Bible regularly. In 1948 G. Bessonov, anxious to convert the masses in the U.S.S.R., suggested to the Society that it prepare a new, more up-to-date, translation; but the Society took the position that another version was unnecessary since both the Orthodox and the Protestants were quite satisfied with Pavsky's translation and do not want another.

X.

RUSSIAN CATHOLICISM

The Ruthenian Uniates

The disintegration of Kievan Russia, which resulted from Mongol invasion, produced great changes in its western principalities, most of which were conquered by the Lithuanians. This obscure but warlike tribe, closely related to the Slavs, was organized into a powerful state, first by Mindovg, who died in 1263, and then by Gedimin, who assumed the title of grand duke of Lithuania in 1316. The Lithuanians were heathen; but Olgierd, Gedimin's son, became Orthodox, married a princess of the house of Moscow, and in 1377 died a monk according to the custom of that house.

Jagello, Olgierd's youngest son, who became the grand duke, married Jadwiga, queen of Poland, in 1386 and became a fervent Roman Catholic. Unable to force his Lithuanian subjects to accept the so-called Union of Krevo, which surrendered to the Polish crown all Lithuanian and Ruthenian (western Russian) lands, Jagello inaugurated instead the process of the gradual Polonization of those lands. Seventy per cent of the population of Lithuania were Ruthenian (Russian) Orthodox, subject to the metropolitan of Kiev, who lived in Moscow, the capital of the rival state; and they could be used by Russian sovereigns to promote their policy. In order to prevent such a thing from happening, the Lithuanian grand dukes very soon began to detach their Orthodox dioceses from Moscow.

Although the Lithuanian grand dukes occasionally succeeded in obtaining for their dioceses a separate primate from the patriarch of Constantinople, whom their dioceses ultimately obeyed, they usually were under the primacy of the metropolitan of Kiev, residing in Moscow. The problem of the Ruthenian churches became exceedingly complicated in the reign of Jagello's son Casimir (1447–1492), when the Act of Union of Florence was signed. While the Muscovites rejected the union outright the Ruthenians were more accommodating. The Ruthenian nobles, already much Polonized, were not in a hurry to quarrel with the Latins.

Cardinal Isidore, metropolitan of Kiev, who signed the Act of Union of Florence, was expelled from Moscow in 1441 but found a friendly reception in Lithuania. In 1448, the Russian bishops assembled in Moscow, elected Jonas, bishop of Ryazan, to succeed Isidore, who went to Rome and then to Constantinople as papal legate. The Ruthenian dioceses of Lithuania and Poland acknowledged the authority of Jonas for ten years. The Roman Curia, engaged elsewhere, did not interfere. In 1458, however, Pope Calixtus III divided the Russian Church into two provinces, leaving that of Moscow to Cardinal Isidore and providing a new primate, Gregory the Bulgarian, Isidore's archdeacon, for that of Lithuania.

The pope-appointed Lithuanian primate, observing the extreme unpopularity of the Union of Florence among the Ruthenians, submitted in 1470 to Dionysius, patriarch of Constantinople. Misael, Gregory's successor, supported for a time the Union of Florence but later changed his mind and died Orthodox. Joseph Bolgarinovich (1498–1501), another primate, acknowledged Pope Alexander VI the supreme head of the Church but could not persuade his subjects to do the same. Still the historical development of Lithuania tended to bring about its fusion with Poland and the ultimate submission of the Ruthenian Church to Rome.[1]

In 1569, by a treaty of Lublin, Poland and Lithuania formed a single state, where the Poles obtained their pre-eminence over the Lithuanians. The Lithuanians were obliged to surrender several rich provinces and generally to take second place. Sigismund August, who accomplished the union, knew that his vast state, inhabited by the Roman Catholics, Orthodox, and Protestants, could not survive unless religious toleration was adopted. He was kind to the Protestants, who multiplied exceedingly in his reign;

the greatest magnates, such as Princes Radziwill and Sapieha, and Chodkiewicz, became Calvinist. Protestant churches began to cover Poland. According to the Jesuit Cihovy, in 1556 only one thousandth part of the Lithuanians really remained Roman Catholic; and in the diocese of Zhmud only six priests remained. Calvinism spread like fire among the Orthodox as well. In the single diocese of Novogrodek 650 churches were closed, and out of 600 gentry families only 16 remained Orthodox.[2]

Poland was reconquered for Rome by the Jesuits, who appeared in the country in 1568. The Jesuits opened several fine colleges to educate children of the nobles and were very successful in converting them. The Jesuits also organized public disputations with the Protestants, which nearly always ended in disaster for the latter. The Unitarians, Calvinists, and Lutherans began, as a rule, to contradict each other and to make fools of themselves. Thanks to the efforts of Fr. Skarga and Fr. Warszawicki the great Protestant nobles began to return to Catholicism.

Encouraged by their success with the Protestants, the Jesuits turned their attention to the Orthodox. They wanted to revive in Poland the Union of Florence, which long ago had died. Fr. Skarga took the initiative and broached the subject in a letter to the great Ruthenian noble, Prince Constantin Ostrozhsky, founder of the Orthodox college and printing press in Ostrog. Unsuccessful in this move, Fr. Skarga found in the quarrel between the Ruthenian Orthodox bishops and the Confraternities another opening. The bishops very often were unworthy men, appointed by the king to their sees for personal and political reasons. Their behavior often was scandalous and unedifying in the extreme. When in 1589 Jeremiah, patriarch of Constantinople, visited Poland, he found the Ruthenian Church in need of radical reform and was obliged to depose not only several priests and bishops but the primate, Metropolitan Onesiphorous Devochka, himself.

Having no confidence in Ruthenian prelates, the patriarch commissioned the Confraternities, a sort of parish guild, the greatest of which was that of Lwów chartered in 1586, to watch over the prelates. Then the patriarch, under strong pressure, consecrated Michael Rohoza as the new primate, although he distrusted him, and appointed Cyril Terlecki, bishop of Lutsk, his exarch to watch over the primate. The Ruthenian prelates were infuriated with these arrangements, which curtailed their privileges and put them under the supervision of the Confraternities.

The only possible way for the bishops to regain their former position was in union with Rome, an arrangement which promised many other political and pecuniary advantages. Gideon Balaban, bishop of Lwów, initiated the movement for union with Rome and he found support in Cyril Terlecki, bishop of Lutsk, and the brilliant Hypatius Pociej, bishop of Brest. These two bishops prepared the Articles of the Union with Rome, which they presented to the king of Poland and Sweden, Sigismund III. The king was a fanatical Roman Catholic who dreamed of making both countries entirely Roman Catholic. The Articles of Union professed submission to the pope but protected Orthodox teaching and rites. They stipulated the suppression of the Confraternities and papal protection against the nobles and the Constantinople authorities in order that they might retain the Church property. Senatorial seats and other privileges also were claimed.

The articles angered the laity, and two bishops refused to sign them. Nevertheless Pociej and Terlecki went to Rome, where Clement VIII proclaimed the Union in 1595. The Ruthenians accepted the decrees of Florence and Trent but preserved their rite and organization.[3] A council at Brest in Poland was convened in 1596 to proclaim the Union. The primate, five bishops, and a few archimandrites attended the council, where the pope and the Polish king were represented by large delegations. The council proclaimed the Union and excommunicated all those who opposed it, and the king confirmed the decree. The Orthodox also staged in Brest their own council in opposition to the Union. Patriarchal Vicar Nicephorus of Constantinople, the celebrated scholar Cyril Loukaris, Luke, metropolitan of Belgrade, two Ruthenian bishops, many archimandrites, two hundred clergy with several nobles and the Confraternities' delegates attended the council, which deposed and excommunicated the primate and his bishops for their betrayal of Orthodoxy.

A long struggle between the Orthodox and the Uniates over the mastery of the Ruthenian Church followed. The Orthodox, particularly Stephen Zizanius, Meletius Smotritsky, and Zakhariah Kopistinsky, attacked the Uniates in their writings. They also, with but little success, tried to form a united front with the Protestants against Rome. Gradually the recalcitrant bishops died while a good many of the clergy submitted to Rome. The great magnates and gentry, anxious for political privileges, deserted the Orthodox in due course. Many townsmen became Polonized. Only the monks and the peasants remained Orthodox.

Orthodoxy was saved from extinction in Poland by the Ukrainian Cossacks. The Cossacks were adventurers, outlaws, and fugitives from Poland and Lithuania, who fled to the rich and empty plains of southern Russia in order to be free and to live by hunting and fighting the Moslems of Crimea. These Cossacks, whose headquarters were in Zaporozhe on the Dnieper, not only expressed social protest but also championed Ruthenian nationality and Orthodox religion.[4] Peter Konashevich-Sahaydachny, the Cossack leader, obtained the restoration of the Orthodox hierarchy in the Ukraine, where it had died out. In 1620, Job Boretsky, abbot of Kiev monastery, was consecrated bishop by Theophanes, patriarch of Jerusalem; and several other bishops also were consecrated.

The Polish Government refused to recognize the new bishops and outlawed them; but the Cossacks obtained a royal decree in 1633 which allowed the Orthodox to have their own bishops. The celebrated theologian, Peter Mohyla, a Rumanian nobleman, archimandrite of Kievo-Pechersky monastery, was made primate in 1633. This great scholar did much for Orthodoxy not only in the Ukraine but generally. He founded the first Orthodox Ecclesiastical Academy (Faculty of Theology) in eastern Europe and wrote the " Confession of Orthodox Faith," an authoritative statement of Orthodox teaching.[5] In 1654 the Ukrainian Cossacks, led by Getman Bohdan Khmelnitsky, rejected Polish overlordship for that of Moscow; and in 1667 the Poles were forced to recognize this change of authority. In 1686 all the Ukrainian dioceses, over which Moscow ruled, joined the Russian patriarchate which they had left in 1458.

The union of the eastern Ukraine with Muscovy was a grievous blow to the Ruthenian Orthodox in Poland, for they lost their primate and several bishops, their Kievan theologians, and their Cossack defenders. Moreover, the Polish Government became highly suspicious toward them, fearing new desertion to Moscow. Several decrees hostile to the Orthodox were published. In 1681 Joseph Shumliansky, bishop of Lwów, became Uniate, and the bishops of Przemyśl and of Lutsk followed him soon after. In 1720 the Uniate primate, Leo Kishka, convened a council in Zamoste, where the Uniate Church was declared the only legal Church in Poland, except the Latin. The spoliation of the Orthodox began. From 1732 to 1743 the Uniates seized 128 Orthodox monasteries and a multitude of parish churches. The Orthodox retained only one diocese, that of Mstislav in White Russia, while nine ancient Ruthenian dioceses became Uniate.

The situation, however, was again about to change in the favor of the Orthodox. The Russian empire was nearing its zenith while Poland was rapidly disintegrating. In order to prevent the use of the Protestant and Orthodox dissenters as a fifth column by Prussia and Russia the Polish diet excluded them from its membership as well as from civil service and the courts. Public worship was proscribed to dissenters. After these restrictions, George Konissky, archbishop of White Russia, came to Moscow in 1764 and related to Catherine II the situation of the Orthodox in Poland. The empress promised to protect the Orthodox, who then numbered 600,000 persons against 4,000,000 of the Uniates. Within a few years the partitions of Poland began, and in 1795 Poland ended its existence as a state.

The partitions of Poland returned all the Ruthenians to Russia, that is, the White Russians and Ukrainians, except those of Galicia and Carpathian Russia. George Konissky, archbishop of White Russia, worked so well among the Uniates, most of whom were only nominally loyal to Rome, that by 1796 over two million of them rejoined the Orthodox Church.[6] Another large group of the Uniates rejoined the Russian Church in the reign of Nicholas I, thanks to the efforts of Count N. Protasov, the high procurator of the Holy Synod (1749–1855), and Joseph Semashko (1798–1868), a White Russian Uniate ecclesiastic. Semashko wanted all the eastern Slavs to form a single Church. By a series of reforms, which he carried out, as the Uniate bishop of Mstislav and Lithuania, he prepared the necessary ground for the reunion of those Uniates with the Russian Church. The union was effected in 1839 in Polotsk, the very city of which Josaphat Kuntsevich, the Uniate martyr, who died in 1623, was the archbishop. There were received into the Russian Church 1,607 parishes with 1,600,000 people.[7] Six hundred Uniate clergymen refused, however, to submit, and about 160 of them persevered in this attitude to the end. Severe repressions were used to force the recalcitrant Uniate clergy and laymen into submission.

After 1839 the only Uniate diocese which remained in Russia was that of Kholm in Russian Poland. It was reunited with the Russian Church in 1875 thanks to the efforts of another Uniate prelate, Marcellus Poppel, dean of Kholm, afterward bishop. Out of 284 priests only a half submitted, while 74 were deported and 66 fled to Austria, which remained the last refuge of the Ruthenian Uniates.[8] When Poland was partitioned Galicia was taken over by Roman Catholic Austria, which did much to improve the social position and education of the Uniate clergy. In 1808 the Austrian Government restored the ancient Galician primacy (first founded in 1371) and attached it to the see of Lwów. The Austrians also promoted the national movement among the Galician Ukrainians, hoping thereby to keep the Poles in check and to attract the sympathy of the Ukrainians in the Russian empire.

The Roman Curia also looked with special attention to Galicia, which could be used as a bridgehead for the conversion to Roman Catholicism of Slavs of the Russian empire. A Ruthenian college was established in Rome in 1897. The Jesuits reorganized the Uniate monks, the Ruthenian rite was purged of accretions, two Galician primates of the nineteenth century, Michael Levitsky and Sylvester Sembratovich were made cardinals. The increase of the trend toward Rome called into being an opposite trend toward the reunion with the Russian Orthodox Church, propounded by the so-called Moscophiles, inspired largely by Archpriest John Naumovich.[9]

The vision of the united Ukraine obedient to Rome and leading the Great Russians themselves toward Rome inspired the last great Uniate primate, Count Andrew Sheptitsky (1864–1944). He dedicated his long life to the realization of this ideal, but circumstances were against him. The Poles, who took over Galicia from Austria in 1920, not only failed to help Sheptitsky but virtually prevented the realization of his dream. They persecuted the Uniates and the Orthodox alike in a futile effort to reduce Ukrainian nationalism. The Poles succeeded only in uniting both Uniates and Orthodox in hatred toward themselves, and as a result a good many Ukrainians welcomed the destruction of Poland by the Germans in World War II.

The Bolsheviks, who defeated the Germans, did not forget that the Ukrainian nationalists were allies of the Nazis. Galicia was the nationalist stronghold and the Uniate Church its backbone; therefore the destruction of that Church was inevitable. In 1945 the Bolsheviks arrested and deported all seven Uniate bishops, including the new primate, Joseph Slipy; and a few days later five hundred priests were deported. Dr. Kostelnik, who wanted to unite the Galicians with the Russian Church, received every encouragement. Dr. Michael Melnik, vicar general of Przemyśl, and Fr. Anthony Pelvetsky, rural dean of Gusiatin, supported him. Every kind of persuasion was used; and by July, 1945, 997 Uniate priests out of 1,270 who still remained in Galicia joined Dr. Kostelnik and his committee.

On March 8, 1946, an assembly of the Uniate clergy was convened in Lwów. Two hundred and sixteen delegates voted for reunion with the Russian Church and reunion was then proclaimed.[10] Although Dr. Kostelnik was murdered in October, 1948, by Ukrainian nationalists in Lwów, his ideal was realized. By 1949 not a single church remained in Uniate hands; all had passed to the Orthodox. The Uniates, however, preserved for a while one diocese in the Soviet Union, that of Mukačevo in Carpathian Russia, an ancient diocese which had joined the Roman Church in 1646. Carpathian Russia was at one time a part of

Hungary and afterward of Czechoslovakia. The Carpathian Uniates always disliked the Latins, and from 1919 to 1935, 120,000 people joined the Orthodoxy and were organized into a diocese, which is now in the Russian patriarchate.[11] The Uniate diocese of Mukačevo ceased to exist on August 28, 1949, when its reunion with the Russian Orthodox Church was proclaimed. The last Uniate bishop, Theodore Romzha, died in mysterious circumstances in 1947 in Mukačevo. (*Zhurnal Moskovskoi Patriarkhii,* October, 1949.)

At present the Ruthenian Uniates survive in organized form only outside the Soviet Union, partly in Czechoslovakia and partly in America, where they number over one million. The American Uniates are descendants of those Ruthenians who migrated to the United States, Canada, and South America. Although they are well organized and on the whole loyal to Rome, in the past a great many of them, once in America, left the Roman Church, and joined the Russian Orthodox Church in America. The Russian Orthodox Church in America now has between 300,000 and 400,000 members, most of whom are descendants of the former Uniates.

The Ruthenian Uniate movement has had a long history during which it has claimed at times a very large constituency of Russian people loyal to Rome. At other times, however, it has lost much of its ground to the Orthodox Church. The Uniates, as a group opposed in loyalty to the Russian Church, should be recognized as real Nonconformists although they retained much of Orthodoxy in rite and belief. Today the Ruthenian Uniates seem to have good prospects for survival in the Americas, and their contemporary significance is that of being a bridge-Church between Roman Catholicism and Orthodoxy.

THE RUSSIAN CATHOLICS

The history of Roman Catholicism among the Great Russians or Muscovites is closely connected with the Society of Jesus. After their success with the union of Brest in Poland, the Jesuits dreamed of a successful union in Muscovy. Antonio Possevino

STATISTICS OF THE RUTHENIAN CATHOLICS

(Communicated in 1948 by His Eminence Cardinal Eugène Tisserant,
Bishop of Porto and Santa Rufina, Secretary to the Sacred
Congregation for Eastern Church)

	Priests	Faithful	Priests	Faithful
I. *In Europe*				
Poland (Galicia)				
Lwów		1,300,000		
Przemyśl		1,159,380		
Stanislawów		1,000,000		
Lemkovshchina		400,000		
Priests for entire Galicia	2,303			
Sub-Carpathia				
Mukačevo	368	461,555		
Miszkolcz	49	36,094		
Preshov	247	141,522		
Jugoslavia				
Crisio	71	100,000		
Total	3,038	4,598,551	3,038	4,598,551
II. *In America*				
United States				
a. Apostolic Exarchate for the Galician Ruthenians (Philadelphia)	133	305,726		
b. Apostolic Exarchate for the Sub-Carpathian Ruthenians (Pittsburgh)	154	278,171		
Canada				
a. Apostolic Exarchate of Central Canada (Winnipeg)	58	150,000		
b. Apost. Exarch. of Western Canada (Edmonton)	44	60,000		
c. Apost. Exarch. of Eastern Canada (Toronto)	32	55,000		
Argentina	6	120,000		
Brazil	18	85,000		
Paraguay		20,000		
Uruguay		10,000		
Venezuela		284		
Peru		87		
Total	445	1,084,268	445	1,084,268
Grand Total:			3,483	5,682,819

had tried to interest Ivan the Terrible in union with Rome but had failed. Later on Jesuits succeeded in obtaining from the false Dimitri a promise to make Russia Uniate; but his assassination in 1606 followed by the Polish invasion and the increased hatred of the Russians toward anything Western ruined all their plans. Not until 1667 did the Muscovites agree to recognize Roman Catholics as Christians. In the reign of Alexis, father of Peter the Great, George Krizhanich, the celebrated Roman Catholic priest from Croatia, came to Russia hoping to promote its union with Rome; but he could achieve nothing.

The Austrians, who usually were the protectors of the Roman Catholics in Muscovite Russia, obtained permission in 1634 to bring a Roman Catholic priest to Moscow to minister to its Catholic inhabitants, all of whom were aliens. In 1685 the Jesuits opened a school and began their usual propaganda among the Russian aristocracy. Although the Jesuits were expelled in 1690, the Russians nevertheless allowed a Roman Catholic church to be built in Moscow; and it was opened at the end of the seventeenth century. The Jesuits, while unable to make direct converts, succeeded nevertheless in greatly influencing the Russian Church through the Ukrainian theologians, nearly all of whom were their pupils at one time or another.

Sylvester Medvedev (1641–1691), abbot of Zaikonospassky monastery in Moscow, was the first Muscovite Latinizer among the clergy although he never was a Roman Catholic himself. A pupil of the celebrated Ruthenian preacher from Poland, Simeon Polotsky, who completed his studies in Jesuit colleges, Medvedev adopted the Latin view of the Blessed Sacrament. He believed that the change of bread and wine into the body and blood of our Lord occurred during the Liturgy at the uttering of the words of institution and not at the recitation of the prayer to the Holy Ghost as the Greeks taught. In 1690 Patriarch Joachim of Moscow convened a council which condemned the Latin view; and although Medvedev recanted, he was executed in 1691 on a political issue. He supported the regent Sophia against her brother, the future Peter the Great.[12]

The Russian Latinizers did not fare well under the great em-

peror Peter, who wanted to reduce the Orthodox Church to the
level of a department of state on the pattern of Hanoverian Anglicanism or Prussian Lutheranism. In the struggle between
Stephen Yavorsky, metropolitan of Ryazan, who opposed Peter's
Erastianism, and Theophanes, archbishop of Pskov, who supported the emperor, Russian Latinizers rallied around Peter's opponents and suffered accordingly as the emperor won his way.
The conflict ended in the reign of Empress Anna (1730–1740),
who was surrounded by Lutheran Germans, her advisers when
she was the duchess of Kurland. Even the chaplain to the Spanish embassy in St. Petersburg, Fr. Ribeira, O.P., took part in
controversies; and his treatise was translated into Russian.

As a result of the struggle, a number of prominent churchmen
were unfrocked and imprisoned. Among the victims were George
Dashkov, metropolitan of Rostov, Leo Yurlov, bishop of Voronezh, Sylvester, metropolitan of Kazan, Varlaam Voinatovich,
archbishop of Kiev, Bishop Ignatius Smola, and three archimandrites. Later the archbishops of Belgorod, Chernigov, Pskov, and
Tver were removed from their sees. None of these prelates ever
was a Roman Catholic, but they all opposed the Protestant Erastianism of Peter the Great and of Anna. Most of them were
Latin-trained and were inspired with Roman ideals about the
proper relationship between Church and State.

In spite of such unfavorable times the Catholics gained a few
aristocratic converts, such as Alexis Ladyzhensky and Prince
Michael Golitsyn. The first illustrious Russian convert, Prince Di-
mitri-Augustin Golitsyn (1770–1840), was a relative of Prince
Michael. Born in The Hague, where his father was the ambassador, Dimitri Golitsyn, was baptized in the Russian Church.
His father, a friend of Diderot and Voltaire, was an atheist while
his mother, Amalie von Schmettau, daughter of the famous
Prussian field marshal, was a Roman Catholic. At the age of
seventeen Dimitri became a Roman Catholic and in 1792 went
as a tourist to America. He soon decided to dedicate his life to
the priesthood and entered St. Mary's Seminary in Baltimore.

Dimitri Golitsyn was the first Catholic clergyman to receive all
his orders in the United States. He is considered, therefore, the

father of the powerful American Catholic clergy. Golitsyn was ordained a priest in 1795 and soon moved to the Alleghenies, where he erected a log church near Mr. McGwire's settlement, where many Catholics lived. His residence was at the site of the present town of Loretto, Pennsylvania. Fr. Golitsyn administered singlehanded the area, which now includes the three vast dioceses of Pittsburgh, Erie, and Harrisburg. Nevertheless, Fr. Golitsyn died as poor as he lived. Not only did he spend all his inheritance on missionary labors but also he contracted large debts, which, however, he was able to repay.[13]

Fr. Golitsyn, although a Russian and a nominal Orthodox when a child, spent all his life outside Russia, where he was hardly known. Russian Catholicism as a group movement began with the reappearance of the Jesuits in Russia. When Clement XIV suppressed the Jesuit Order in 1773, Catherine II refused to dissolve the Jesuits in the Russian empire and allowed them to continue their activities. At that time the Jesuits numbered about two hundred, most of them living in White Russia. Paul I, Catherine II's son, believed himself to be a defender of Christianity against the atheism of the French Revolution; and the Jesuits found in him an ally. The emperor issued a new *règlement* for the Jesuits, making them independent from the Roman Catholic hierarchy of the empire. He also restored their estates to them and permitted them to open schools and institutions. Finally, he obtained from Pius VII a brief *Catholico Fidei,* which restored the Society of Jesus in Russia.[14]

Alexander I, who succeeded Paul, was for a long time friendly to the Jesuits, who greatly increased in numbers. The Government permitted them to open missions in the provinces of Saratov, Astrakhan, Riga, and elsewhere. In 1812 the Jesuit College in Polotsk was made a university with four faculties. The sudden death of Fr. Paul Gruber, head of the Jesuits in Russia and confidant of two emperors, was a serious loss to them, particularly since the new chief, Fr. Berezowski, lacked the charm of his predecessor. The order in Russia was ruined, however, by the successful activities of a brilliant French Jesuit, Fr. Rozaven, who began to make many aristocratic converts. He persuaded Prince

Alexis Golitsyn with his sister, Catherine, Countess Rastopchin, Countess Nicholas Tolstoy and others to join the Roman Church. The conversions of the young Prince Alexander Golitsyn, nephew of the Minister of Cults, Princess Elisabeth Golitsyn, and Madame Svechin followed soon after.

The Government replied with a decree on December 20, 1815, which expelled the Jesuits from both Russian capitals. Five years later the Jesuits were expelled from the empire altogether, their schools closed, and their estates handed over to the Roman Catholic bishops. Among the Jesuit converts Sophia Svechin was most remarkable. Born in 1782, daughter of Secretary of State Peter Soimonov, she was married at the age of seventeen to middle-aged General Svechin with whom she was not happy. Mixing with the French *émigrés* in St. Petersburg, she became attracted to Catholicism and on November 8, 1815, was received into the Roman Church by Fr. Rozaven.[15]

A few months later Mme. Svechin left Russia for Paris, where she started her celebrated salon, which attracted many eminent Frenchmen of clerical and royalist views. A chapel was consecrated at Mme. Svechin's house and many great French priests celebrated Mass there. She died in 1854, leaving interesting papers. Mme. Svechin converted to Catholicism a young Russian diplomat, Prince Ivan Gagarin (1814–1882), who became a Jesuit.[16] He, together with another Russian Jesuit, Ivan Martynov, founded the celebrated Slavonic Library in Paris. Their pupils, Fr. Paul Pierling, S.J., and Fr. M. J. Rouet de Journel, published many learned books on Russian history.

Neither Prince Dimitri Golitsyn nor Mme. Svechin made much impression on Russian society, but Peter Chaadaev (1793–1856) did. This Russian aristocrat, educated at Moscow University, fought in the Russian Army during the Napoleonic Wars. He was a Freemason for a while and also belonged to secret revolutionary societies which aimed to change the regime in Russia. He was, however, abroad during the Decembrist rebellion in 1825 and therefore was not implicated in it. In 1836 he published the celebrated *Philosophical Letters,* which declared that Russia had neither a past nor a present and that so-called Russian culture was merely an aping of the West. According to Chaadaev the root of Russian misfortunes lay in the fact that Russia received its Christianity not from vigorous Rome but from decadent Byzantium. In order to realize its mission in the world Russia must enter spiritually into the western European family of nations. Unity is the very essence of Christianity and the papacy is its symbol. Chaadaev called Rome the living center of Christendom and claimed that all Christian Churches apart from Rome were defective; nevertheless, he did not become a Catholic. He died Orthodox in 1856, and the Russian Government declared him a lunatic.[17] Professor V. S. Pecherin, of Moscow University, who developed views similar to those of Chaadaev, was more logical. He left Russia and became a Redemptorist, spending his life successfully fighting Protestantism in Ireland. Like Chaadaev, Pecherin considered the Reformation a tragedy for the West because it broke its unity.[18]

Vladimir Soloviev (1853–1901) was the first Russian Catholic who objected both to the adoption of the Latin rite by the Russian Catholics and to their denationalization. He wanted them to be united with Rome while preserving their rite and traditions. Son of a great Russian historian, Sergius Soloviev, Vladimir Soloviev was a brilliant philosopher and religious thinker who greatly influenced Russian religious thought. Educated at Moscow University, Soloviev also attended lectures at the Ecclesiastical Academy. In 1874 he published *The Crisis of Western Philosophy,* in which he attacked positivism and declared that there can be no progress unless faith and reason are reconciled. In 1875 Soloviev went to London and Egypt to study mystical and esoteric religions and sects. He was an opponent of capital punishment and requested Alexander III in 1881 to pardon the assassins of his father, Emperor Alexander II, but his request was denied. By this time Soloviev already had published some important papers; and when he was disappointed in imperial Russia's failure to realize his theocratic dreams, Soloviev turned to the West.

The ideas of a Croat priest of the seventeenth century, George Krizhanich, who visualized the union of all Slavonic nations under the leadership of Muscovy united with Rome, fired Soloviev's

imagination. He went to Croatia and discussed the matter with
its celebrated Roman Catholic bishop, Mgr. Strossmayer. As a
result of his conversations with the Croatian Catholics, Soloviev
published two important books: *Istoriia i budushchnost teokratii*
(*The History and Future of Theocracy*), in which he advocated
the union of all Western and Eastern Christians under the paternal authority of the pope, and *La Russie et l'Église Universelle,*
in which he proposed to achieve reunion through an alliance for
this purpose between the pope and the czar.[19] It is difficult to sum
up Soloviev's philosophy in a few words. He absorbed much from
the teaching of Böhme, a German mystic, who greatly influenced
Kuhlmann and often was very near pantheism.

According to Soloviev a divine principle lies at the basis of the
world as the Creator and the triune God. Being, activity, and
consciousness are the three sides of the divine nature. In the full-
ness of the one divine nature there is also an antidivine element
— plurality, chaos. God, however, restrains it. In order to overcome chaos and to reduce it to eternal nonbeing, God ceases to
suppress chaos within himself and thus the world appears as
something opposed to God. The history of the world consists in
the gradual penetration of the world by the divine principle. God
first introduces into the world mechanical unity, then dynamic,
and afterward organic unity. Finally man is created to be united
with God freely, perfectly, and mutually. The trinitarian principle is incarnated in mankind in the form of three elements:
man, woman, and society. The three fruits of the divine penetration of the world are perfect man — Christ; perfect woman — the
mother of God; and perfect society — the Church. In order to
complete the union of mankind with God, the Church must
penetrate secular society. For this goal the Church needs the co-
operation of the State. The historical mission of Russia is to provide the Catholic Church with the political power which is
needed to save Europe and the world. The pope and the emperor
must form an alliance.[20] Soloviev defined the Church as " a living
and self-conscious being, possessing moral freedom, working for
its self-realization, a true bride of God, forming with him a full
and perfect unity, indwelt by him entirely — in one word as

Sophia, the divine Wisdom." [21]

Soloviev's teaching on Sophia, strangely reminiscent of the Dukhobors', impressed several Russian religious thinkers, including Prince Sergius Trubetskoy, Fr. Paul Florensky, Fr. Sergius Bulgakov, and Nicholas Berdyaev. Soloviev believed that the existence of a personal God implies that the world has also a personality, which he called Sophia and pictured as a beautiful woman. Soloviev's teaching on morality, sex, society, war, and punishment was original and paradoxical. Vladimir Soloviev was received into the Roman Church by Fr. Nicholas Tolstoy, a Russian Catholic priest of the Byzantine rite in Moscow, in 1896. Soloviev believed himself to belong to both Churches at once. He never formally recanted Orthodoxy and he died in communion with it in 1901. Fr. Beliaev, an Orthodox priest, administered him the last sacraments. [22]

Fr. Nicholas Tolstoy, who received Soloviev into the Roman Church, continued his activities in Russia. Count Andrew Sheptitsky, the Uniate primate of Galicia, assumed in 1900 the supervision of the Russian Catholics of the Byzantine rite, and gradually some priests and theological students of Soloviev's views entered into contact with Sheptitsky and joined the Roman Church. In 1907 Pius X granted to Sheptitsky patriarchal authority over Russia with the charge to organize the Russian Catholics. In 1908 Sheptitsky himself came to Russia, and in 1909 the first Russian Catholic chapel was opened in St. Petersburg. Fr. Eustace Susalev, a converted Priestist clergyman whose orders Rome recognized as valid, was the rector. Gradually other parishes were opened in Russia for the Catholics of the Byzantine rite, and Fr. Leonid Fedorov, formerly a student at the Orthodox Ecclesiastical Academy in St. Petersburg, was appointed by Rome its exarch in Russia. [23]

The Soviet Revolution ruined the Russian Catholics. The Convent of the Dominican nuns in Moscow, supervised by Mother Catherine Abrikosov, was closed. Fr. Potapii Emelianov, who converted many peasants in southern Russia, disappeared. Finally the exarch himself was arrested in 1922 and charged with anti-Soviet activities. He died in prison a few years later. All other

Russian Catholic priests were gradually imprisoned, and Russian Catholicism was once more suppressed.

Russian Catholicism survived abroad, however, in France, Belgium, Italy, Argentina, the Far East, and the United States. In the latter they have two churches, one of which is a chapel on Mulberry Street in New York. In due course Rome appointed a Lithuanian Marianist, Peter Buchis, the first bishop for the Russian Catholics. Their congregations are small and cannot be called dynamic. The Russians usually are very suspicious of anyone and anything connected with the pope, whom they traditionally believe to be a foreign potentate who has tried many times to enslave their country. The Russian Catholics abroad have failed thus far to produce anyone similar to Prince Dimitri Golitsyn in holiness or to Soloviev in intellectual strength. They have, however, some outstanding leaders, such as Dom Climent Lialin, O.S.B., monk of Amay in Belgium, editor of *Irénikon;* Miss Hélène Iswolsky; and Dr. Irene Posnoff.

The Russian Catholics were always a small, highly educated and rather denationalized group. They hardly influenced the Russian clergy or the Russian masses. The Russian clergy, nevertheless, were influenced powerfully by Latin schoolmen, Latin seminaries, and Latin language. Indeed for a very long time the spiritual formation and professional training of the Russian clergy were nearly the same as those of the Roman Catholic. For all that, the Russian clergy were to thank or to blame the Ukrainian prelates, who ruled them in the eighteenth century.

Today there seems to be no reason for believing that Roman Catholicism will play an important role in the movement of Russian Nonconformity in the near future.

XI.

NEW NONCONFORMITY

The Synodal Regime and Its Opponents

Peter the Great, when he began actually to rule Russia in 1689, realized that Russia was a big but backward country unable to overcome the Swedes and the Turks who barred the way to the open sea and to steady progress. Therefore he decided to reorganize his country on the Western pattern and proceeded to remake the Russian Army, to reorganize the civil service, and to lay foundations for the Russian Navy. He also promoted greatly Russian industry and trade. He hated the old Muscovite way of life, and despised the old-fashioned clergy and the Raskolniks. He preferred to mix freely with foreign adventurers, and he adopted their coarse behavior and manners to such an extent that both the dignified Moscow aristocracy and the masses of the people were shocked. Patriarch Joachim tried in vain to restrain Peter's enthusiasm for Western ways; and when he died the young czar promoted Adrian, the pious but insignificant metropolitan of Kazan, to the patriarchal throne. Adrian died in 1700, and no new patriarch was elected. Peter merely appointed Stephen Yavorsky, metropolitan of Ryazan, to be a locum tenens.

Yavorsky was born in Poland in 1658 and was educated in Jesuit colleges and universities at Kiev and later in Poland. He became a Uniate, under the name of Stanislas; for in that period practically all the Orthodox Greeks, Syrians, and Ukrainians who studied in Roman Catholic universities turned Uniate for a while in order to gain admission. The Jesuits greatly impressed Yavorsky, who remained their admirer and acted as a Latinizer among the Orthodox. After returning to Kiev and to Orthodoxy, Yavor-

sky in quick succession became a monk, a professor at the academy, and in 1700 the metropolitan of Ryazan. Within a few
months after becoming metropolitan, Peter, who liked Yavorsky's
Western sympathies, made him locum tenens of the patriarchal
throne.

Peter, however, was not long in discovering that Yavorsky's
sympathies really were not the same as his own. Peter was a freethinker who early had lost all respect for the old traditions, the
icons, the relics, and the fasts. Elaborate Byzantine rites and ancient monasteries seemed to him either superstitious or useless, or
both. Peter ridiculed the ecclesiastical rites, never kept fasts, and
habitually transgressed all the conventions of his age. To the
Muscovite hierarchy and the Ukrainian Latinizers alike Peter
was most objectionable, and the Raskolniks looked upon him as
the Antichrist. The emperor was fully informed about the opposition that he had stirred up, and he took precautions to prevent
the clergy from allying with other opponents, who hoped to
abolish his reforms. These precautions took the form of new legislation copied from Swedish, Prussian, and English laws of establishment, which was designed to subjugate the Church to the
State.

A Ukrainian theologian, Theophanes Prokopovich (1681–1736),
a brilliant but unscrupulous scholar and statesman with Protestant sympathies, came forward to help the emperor.[1] Prokopovich
was a native of Kiev, and like Yavorsky he studied there and later
went to Poland where he turned Uniate. He completed his studies in Rome, where the Jesuits urged him to join their society.
Prokopovich, however, unlike Yavorsky, despised the Jesuits and
the Roman Church as survivals of barbarism and bigotry. He
frankly welcomed the Reformation and was an unashamed Eras-
tian. Peter was delighted to discover such a man and in 1718
made him bishop of Pskov with a special mission to reorganize
the Russian Church.

By imperial decree the patriarchate of Moscow was abolished
in 1721 and the Holy Governing Synod established to rule the
Russian Church. Neither the bishops nor the clergy nor the
Church laity were consulted. Indeed Prokopovich stated in his

Rozysk, published in St. Petersburg in 1721, that the emperor was the bishop of bishops, called to rule the Church and the State alike. The synod was established solely by imperial decree as an organ of the imperial power and was similar to various other " collegiums " or " ministries " organized at the same time. The emperor was represented in the synod by a lay officer called the Oberprokurator or high procurator. The procurator did not vote, but he submitted to the synod the matters to be discussed, and its acts were not valid unless he countersigned them. Prokopovich fixed the membership of the synod at twelve members: bishops, archimandrites, and archpriests, appointed by the emperor and removable by him at will.

Yavorsky, who was appointed president of the synod, opposed the new regime until his death in 1722. With the rise of the synodal regime Yavorsky's followers, the Ukrainian Latinizers, and the old-fashioned Muscovites began their long struggle with Prokopovich, which ended in their destruction as described above in the discussion of Russian Catholicism.[2] The accession of Empress Elizabeth to the throne in 1741 inspired two of Yavorsky's pupils, Ambrosius Yushkevich, archbishop of Novgorod, and Arsenius Matseievich, metropolitan of Siberia, to present to the empress both in 1742 and in 1744 memorandums which urged her to abolish the " Spiritual *Règlement,*" Prokopovich's legislation, and to re-establish the patriarchate and to protect the Church estates against the Government's plans to take them over. As a minimum improvement the petitioners asked for a reform of the synod to exclude priests from its membership and to make its president the true primate with the title of metropolitan of Moscow and St. Petersburg. Elizabeth left both memorandums unanswered.[3]

The subjugation of the Church to the State continued; and in 1763 Empress Catherine II signed a decree which transferred to the State the endowments of the bishoprics, deaneries, monasteries, and many parishes. In return the State promised to pay to the dispossessed a fixed regular salary, but this promise usually was badly kept. The monasteries were worst hit, and 496 of them were closed outright. Only one half of the monasteries for men

(318) and one third for women (67) were allowed to remain. No monastery was allowed to have more than 33 monks, and no convent was allowed more than 101 nuns. The monastic estates affected by the new decree involved a significant portion of Russian life. According to V. Andreev (*Raskol i ego znachenie v narodnoi russkoi istorii,* page 105) the monastic estates in 1764 were inhabited by 310,000 serfs. Holy Trinity monastery near Moscow alone had over 120,000 serfs, and the Kievan monasteries possessed more than 50,000. All the confiscated estates either were sold by the Government or distributed as grants among court dignitaries.

The spoliation of the Church estates deprived the hierarchy and the monasteries of their influence and increased the grip of the State on the Church. There was no patriarch to protest, and the synod was packed with the crown's nominees. Only Arsenius Matseievich, now metropolitan of Rostov, protested against the increasing State interference in Church affairs. He preached against the secularization of ecclesiastical estates and composed a " rite of anathematizing of those who rob and persecute God's churches and monasteries." For this boldness Arsenius was first deposed and then unfrocked and imprisoned in Reval fortress, where he died in 1772.[4]

With the deposition and imprisonment of Arsenius, the opposition to the synodal regime within the Church was broken for many decades. The Russian aristocracy and gentry who could have led the opposition benefited too much from the imperial regime to fight it and became too indifferent to religion to fight for it. Masses of the people remained inarticulate, while almost the only leadership available was from among the Raskolniks. The history of the Russian Church in the eighteenth century makes painful reading. The record reveals more shadow than light as it recounts the suppression of the patriarchate, the enslavement of the bishops, the spoliation of the Church lands, the oppression of the clergy by Government and nobles alike, and the contempt for the Church in cultured society. Not until the days of the learned Plato Levshin, metropolitan of Moscow (1737–1812) did the Russian Church begin to rise again. Levshin was the first prelate who dared to write his treatises in Russian instead of Latin or Slavonic; and his work *The Orthodox Doctrine,* which appeared in 1765, was translated into eight languages, including English. He favored a return to the old Muscovite traditions and was much interested in the Raskolniks.

In the reign of Alexander I (1801–1825), however, the Russian Church suffered another setback. Alexander, a mystic and Pan-Christian, believed that the essence of religion consisted in communion of the soul with God; and he held that all religions equally lead to God. He felt that the important thing was not abstract dogma but a Christlike life. Consequently the emperor respected equally the Russian monks and sectarians, the French Jesuits and English Quakers, and the German Pietists and the Ruthenian Uniates. He believed in a great invisible Church of the saints of God which includes all the visible Christian churches. These imperial views were reflected in the creation of the Ministry of Cults and Public Education, in 1817. The establishment of the new ministry reduced the synod to an insignificant division presided over by Prince A. Golitsyn, a mystic of the emperor's type. Such a disregard for Orthodoxy by the Government soon produced a strong reaction led by Photius Spassky, archimandrite of Novgorod Yuriev monastery. Supported by Seraphinus Glagolev, metropolitan of St. Petersburg, and Count Andrew Arakcheev, war minister, Photius obtained in 1824 the abolition of the Ministry of Cults and the dismissal of Prince Golitsyn.

The humiliation of the Church under Golitsyn produced two important results: the appearance of the so-called lay theologians and the change of the policy of the Government toward the Church. Alexis Khomiakov (1809–1860), a wealthy nobleman, was the first lay theologian. He disapproved the aping of the West and urged the return to native traditions. The Church was for Khomiakov a free union of the faithful in truth and love — not a department of state nor a creature of doctrine. He believed that all the forms of Western Christianity were wrong because they were based ultimately on rationalism. The Roman Church externalized the infallible authority in the papacy; and under the necessity of justifying itself before logical reason, it unavoidably became rationalist. Protestantism, on the other hand, based itself on private judgment and soon degenerated into a multitude of warring sects which contributed to religious indifferentism and unbelief. The Orthodox Church, according to Khomiakov, has no external authority, but it is the truth itself and needs no evidence from the outside. He held that the emperor was only the defender of the Russian Church and never actually its head.[5]

Nicholas I, who succeeded Alexander I as emperor in 1825, was quite a different man. He thought of the Russian Church as a bulwark of monarchy against corroding Western influences; and he adopted Count Uvarov's celebrated formula for Russia: Orthodoxy, Autocracy, Nationalism. This formula demanded the utmost state support for the Orthodox Church, paternal bureaucracy, and the pre-eminence of the Great Russians over everyone else in the empire. The clergy were to educate the masses in the proper spirit, and in order to perform that function they needed to be better educated and financially independent. The old-fashioned system of education of the clergy in Latin, borrowed from the Jesuit Colleges of the seventeenth century, was changed. Kazan Academy and many new seminaries were opened, and thirteen new dioceses were founded. The State began to pay the salaries of the clergy and to promote missions at home and abroad. In return the Church was expected to support the imperial regime, which retained its old grip on the Church. In the reign of Alexander II (1855–1881), who liberated Russian serfs and reformed the courts, the Army, and the local governments, two Russian prelates made an effort to secure more freedom for the Church. Agathangelus Soloviev, archbishop of Volhynia, and Innocent Popov-Veniaminov, metropolitan of Moscow, appealed to the czar requesting him to convene the Russian National Church Council in order to abolish certain uncanonical regulations forced on the Church by Peter I and his successors and to effect some needed reforms. Nevertheless, even such a liberal sovereign as Alexander II did not feel that he could release the Church, which had become such a useful tool in influencing the popular masses.

The disintegration of the imperial regime which had begun in the reign of Alexander I progressed steadily under his brother and nephew. The efforts of Alexander III and his minister, Professor C. Pobedonostsev, who used the Church to the full to prop up the regime, failed. The empire collapsed in the reign of Nicholas II (1894–1917). Permission to convene the Russian National Church Council never was granted. Although the synod itself petitioned the emperor in 1905 to convene the council, only a special commission to study the matter was authorized. By this time a good many radicals had appeared in the clergy, and they demanded sweeping reforms in the Church itself, including the promotion of married priests to bishoprics. Several priests took part in revolutionary activities, and Fr. Tikhanovsky, Fr. Petrov, Fr. Anastasev, and the unfortunate Fr. Gapon belonged to this group.[6]

Toward the end of the synodal regime (1900) the Russian Church was divided into 65 dioceses with 65 diocesan and 40 auxiliary bishops. There were 48,000 churches, of which 37,000 were parochial, and 19,000 chapels and prayer houses. These churches were served by about 45,000 priests, 15,000 deacons, and 44,000 lay readers. Among the parochial clergy 23,000 received their salaries from the state. There were 500 monasteries with 8,000 monks and 7,000 novices and 300 convents with 9,000 nuns and 29,000 novices. The clergy were trained in 185 preparatory schools with 32,000 pupils, 58 seminaries with 20,000 students, and four academies (more advanced theological schools) with 1,000 students. The clergy directed 22,000 primary schools with 600,000 pupils besides 19,000 parish schools with 900,000 pupils.[7] The monasteries maintained 200 hospitals and 150 houses for the aged; and there were, besides, 100 parochial hospitals and 1,000 houses for the aged.

Although the Russian Church certainly was enslaved by the State during the synodal period, it was by no means dead. Indeed, it developed an impressive missionary program, produced many saints, theologians, and philosophers, and carried out ever-increasing cultural and charitable activities.[8] Insofar as it kept alive its true character and functions as a Church and refused to conform absolutely to the State ideal and norm for the Church as an agent and tool of the Government, Russian Orthodoxy joined the columns of Nonconformity. In the years ahead it was to stand in great need of those traditions of freedom which it had been able to preserve.

THE RUSSIAN CHURCH AND THE SOVIET REVOLUTION

The overthrow of the empire in 1917 and the disappearance of State supervision left the hierarchy free to reorganize the Church. At that time grave inner conflicts, which subsequently disturbed the Russian Church, were centered around the problem of how the Church should be reorganized and what its relations with the State should be. The bishops faced a formidable task, a task for which neither they, the clergy, nor the laity were prepared, when they took up the problem of reorganization. In all of their thinking the Orthodox emperor had been the defender of the faith, the protector of the Church, and its cornerstone. Without the emperor, they did not know what to do.

The provisional liberal government, which succeeded the empire, at once allowed the convocation of the National Council of the Russian Church. The council opened its sessions on August 15, 1917, and 546 delegates, representing all the Russian dioceses and missions, attended. Ten metropolitans, 17 archbishops, 53 bishops, 15 archimandrites, and 72 archpriests represented the clergy, while 11 titled noblemen, 10 generals, 132 civil servants together with 22 landowners, 69 intellectuals, and several workers, businessmen, and peasants sat among the laity.[9] The majority of the council were conservative, but it also included an important radical minority. The conservatives were led by Anthony Khrapovitsky, archbishop of Kharkov, who wanted the re-establishment of the patriarchate with an autocratic patriarch like Nikon or Hermogen unencumbered with a multitude of advisory committees and control commissions. The radicals, led by Professor B. V. Titlinov, an admirer of Prokopovich, opposed the revival of the patriarchate as a new tyranny. In the end the conservatives won the battle, and the patriarchate was restored on October 30, 1917, by a vote of 141 to 112. The winning majority, however, constituted a mere fourth of the council as so many were absent.[10]

The pious but insignificant president of the council, Tychon (Tikhon) Belavin, metropolitan of Moscow, was elected patriarch; and the council passed a long resolution stating that the Orthodox Church, being the religion of the majority, must be recognized as a privileged body and its canons respected by the State. The council further demanded that the head of the Russian State and the Minister of Cults be Orthodox and that the Church be allowed to teach in schools and to have chaplains in the armed forces. The Communist State answered this resolution with a series of decrees which culminated in a directive on January 23, 1918, which separated the Church from the State and the schools and deprived the Church of all juridical rights. The State proceeded to confiscate all the property of the Church and abolished all chaplaincies in the armed forces, prisons, hospitals, and elsewhere. All State subsidies were taken away from the Church; and the clergy were declared nonproletarian and, as such, deprived of full citizenship. With this one stroke the clergy lost the rights to vote and to be elected to the Soviets, to send their children to certain schools, to settle in certain districts, and to have the usual food rations. In fact they were outlawed.[11] On January 19, 1918, the patriarch in his turn named the Bolsheviks monsters of the human race and destroyers of the Church and excommunicated all those Orthodox who co-operated with them. The council endorsed the patriarch's proclamation and prepared an elaborate plan of resistance to the Bolsheviks. Thus the struggle between the Church and the Revolution began.

The civil war delayed the Soviet attack on the Church; but persecution started in earnest in February, 1922, with the Soviet decree prescribing the seizure of the sacred vessels and reliquaries of the Church to be used for the Famine Fund. The patriarch ordered his clergy to resist the decree, and as a result there were 1,414 cases of resistance and mob violence. The saintly Benjamin Kazansky, metropolitan of Petrograd, headed a group of 45 clergymen who were shot as ringleaders of the resistance; and 250 others, including the patriarch himself, were imprisoned. Thereupon the radical priests, who had founded the Union of the Democratic Clergy in 1917 and resisted the revival of the patriarchate at the council of Moscow, seized the opportunity to capture the central government of the Church in order to reform it according to their ideas. They wanted a close co-operation with the Soviet regime, the abolition of the patriarchate in favor of councils made up of clergy and laity, the accession of married clergy to the office of bishop, and the carrying out of some liturgical reforms.

On May 12, 1922, three priests, Alexander Vvedensky, Eugene Belkov, and Sergius Kalinovsky, went to see the imprisoned patriarch and urged him to resign immediately and to convene a new Church council. The priests also asked the patriarch to re-open the Church chancery. The patriarch agreed to transfer the administration of the Church for the time being to Agathangelus, the metropolitan of Yaroslavl. With the patriarchal letter in their hands, the radicals communicated with the metropolitan and invited him to join them in their plot. The metropolitan refused and was deported to Siberia by the Bolsheviks, who were eager to help the radicals in order to weaken the Russian Church. The radicals, in turn, promised the utmost support of the Government. In 1923 the radicals, who first styled themselves the " Living Church " and then the " Renovators " (Obnovlentsy), held a council in Moscow. At that time they repealed the patriarchal excommunication of the Bolsheviks, deposed and unfrocked the patriarch, and issued several decrees to put into effect their program of reforms.[12] Out of 97 diocesan bishops only 37 accepted the Renovators' program; 36 opposed it, and 24 remained silent. To clear the field, the Renovators forcibly retired 80 prelates and left only 15 to occupy their sees. To take the place of the retired bishops, the Renovators consecrated their own men. The masses of churchmen, however, disliked the Renovators and their reforms; and once the imprisoned patriarch learned of that fact, he decided to regain his freedom even at the cost of recanting his anti-Soviet policy. He made his recantation in a petition to the Soviet Government on June 16, 1923, and the Bolsheviks freed him.

The liberation of the patriarch was a great blow to the Renovators, and after he was freed their decline was rapid. In 1925 they claimed 12,593 parishes, divided into 108 dioceses and served by 192 bishops and 16,540 clergy. In 1927 there were only 84 dioceses, 6,245 parishes, 104 bishops and 10,815 clergy.[13] The Renovators retained only 2,876 parishes in 1936, and in 1943 a movement arose among them to return to the Russian Church. The first prelate to submit was Archbishop Andrew Rastorguev, who was received back only as a priest, the office which he held before becoming a Renovator. The Russian Church rejected altogether the validity of the Renovator orders; and Bishop Sergius Larin, Metropolitan Tikhon Popov, and Archbishop Peter Turbin made their way back into the Russian Church. After the Renovator primate, Metropolitan Vitalius Vvedensky, made his submission, the remaining leaders followed him; and the Renovators disappeared.[14]

Patriarch Tychon died on April 7, 1925, after having appointed three locum tenens to succeed him. None of them, however, was able to take over the charge; and circumstances forced Sergius Starogorodsky (1867–1944), metropolitan of Nizhnii Novgorod, who was for a time a Renovator, to assume the headship of the Russian Church. He had two problems to solve: how to find a *modus vivendi* with the Soviet Government and how to liquidate the Renovator schism. These problems he succeeded ultimately in solving, but not without much suffering and trouble. Sergius' decision to co-operate with the atheist Government shocked many churchmen and produced a strong reaction. Several distinguished prelates imprisoned by the Bolsheviks in the great Solovki monastery in the White Sea sketched their own plan of reconciliation between the Church and the State in a memorandum which they addressed to the Soviet Government in 1926. They demanded full religious freedom including that of propaganda, the liberation of all bishops and clergy arrested at the request of the Renovators, and the cessation of State support of the Renovators. The illustrious archbishop Hilarion Troitsky, Archbishop Pitirim Krylov and Bishop Emanuel Lemeshevsky, later archbishop of Chkalov, were among the signatories. As a matter of fact Sergius' co-operation with the Soviet Government was repudiated by nearly all Russian clergy abroad and by many within the Soviet Union. The leader of the opposition to co-operation with the Government, Joseph Petrovich, metropolitan of Leningrad, eventually was shot by the Bolsheviks as a counterrevolutionary.

Sergius succeeded in obtaining permission in 1927 to establish the patriarchal synod in order to reorganize the Church. His efforts were frustrated, however, by the activities of the Soviet-supported Godless Movement, which aimed to destroy the Church by antireligious propaganda.[15] An old Bolshevik, Emelianus Yaroslavsky, was charged with the direction of the Godless Movement; and he began his activities in 1926 with 2,421 cells and 465,438 members. In 1932 there were 80,000 cells including 7,000,000 adults and 1,500,000 children.[16] The country was flooded with antireligious books, papers, and plays; and profane museums were opened. In spite of the fact that Churches were closed by the thousands, however, the movement failed. It was not easy to get the masses of the people to accept atheism.

Beginning in 1936 Stalin started to look for an agreement with the Church, and the outbreak of the Second World War spurred him to this end. On September 4, 1943, Stalin granted an audience to the aged metropolitan Sergius, accompanied by Metropolitans Nicholas Yarushevich and Alexis Simansky; and on this occasion he intimated that the prelates might convene the National Church Council and elect a patriarch. Consequently on September 8, 1943, twenty-three bishops who still occupied their sees, although their offices at that time mostly involved only nominal responsibilities, met and elected Sergius to the patriarchate. Sergius, however, died on May 15, 1944, after occupying his new post for less than a year. Thereafter Patriarch Alexis was elected on February 1, 1945, by a council attended by 44 bishops and 126 clerical and lay delegates. Three Orthodox patriarchs and representatives of nearly all the Orthodox Churches throughout the world attended the ceremony. Not since 1667 had so many great Orthodox prelates been seen in Moscow, and with the pomp of this occasion the third Rome idea began again to be revived. After a period of severe persecution, the Russian Church emerged again as a significant institution. It seemed to have survived the Communist onslaught.

In a very real sense the Orthodox Church today may be considered the largest "Nonconformist" body in Russia. Certainly the "official" state religion of Russia is Marxist-Leninism; and all Christian groups, both Orthodox and non-Orthodox, are nonconformist in relation to the established faith. Phillips M. Price, Liberal member of the British House of Commons, who visited Russia in 1946, has stated that from a quarter to a third of the Russian population go to church, while about one third profess Marxism. The balance of the population does not adhere actively to either faith but tends to support Communism insofar as it offers concrete advantages. The strength of Orthodoxy is in the Russian masses; but the devotees of the new religion are to be found for the most part among the bureaucrats of higher degrees, senior military officers, Soviet managers and intellectuals, and, of course, the Communists proper.[17] There can be no doubt that Marxism is actually a new religion. As Kingsley Martin, leftist editor of the *New Statesman and Nation* (London), has said: " It has its sacred books, its dogma and philosophy, its library of disputation, its martyrs and heretics. The gospel is spread by a single party whose methods and discipline remind one forcibly of the Jesuit Order. Its object is to substitute science and Marxian order for revelation and clerical control." [18]

When the Soviet Government acknowledged officially the existence of the Russian Church in 1943, it created a special organ to deal with the Church. This organ is known as the Council for the Affairs of the Orthodox Church, and its president, George Karpov, has ministerial rank. He has his representatives all over the Soviet Union, but how far he corresponds to the imperial high procurator it is difficult to say. Officially he is merely a State agent to consider Church requests, and it must be admitted frankly that since the legalization of the Church its position has much improved.

Major General Richard Hilton, D.S.O., M.C., who was the British military attaché in Moscow after the last war and only recently retired, gives some interesting information in the chapter on " Christianity and Communism " in his recent book *Military Attaché in Moscow* (Hollis and Carter, London, 1949). The general does not believe that Christianity and Communism ever can be reconcileᴅ. He understands Communism to be not an abstract theory but the well-defined teaching of Karl Marx and Friedrich Engels, developed by Lenin and Stalin, which is now applied in the Soviet Union and in the countries of its allies and associates. Theistic religion and dialectical materialism are irreçoncilable.

Mr. Hilton admits that churches in Moscow are overcrowded and that besides the poorest classes of the Soviet society, who fill churches in daylight, the well-dressed folk appear at the night services. An atmosphere of the deepest and most moving religious devotion is obvious in Soviet churches. Vast masses are still deeply religious in the U.S.S.R. The general believes that the Soviet Government legalized religion after decades of fierce persecution for three reasons. The Government realized that it is impossible to eradicate religion by persecution. It hopes that religion will die naturally, thanks to the godless school. The general himself does not think so. Enough religious teaching goes from parents to children to prevent such a thing's happening. The second reason, which obliged the Government to stop the persecution of the Orthodox in the Soviet Union, is the desire to please the present masses of the satellite countries, which are deeply religious and will be dismayed with tales of the bloody religious persecution going on in Russia. The third possible reason for the Soviet leniency toward the Orthodox is, according to Hilton, the use of the Russian patriarchate as a tool to promote a reform movement in order to restore Christianity to its humanistic moralism and to destroy Roman Catholicism, which is the strongest bulwark of the Western way of life. The third Rome theory is very convenient in this connection. The position of all churchmen in the Soviet Union, and of the Russian Orthodox prelates particularly, is very delicate. The latter obtained a measure of toleration and even of protection for the all-out support of the regime. So long as aims of the Government and of the Church do not clash, mutual understanding and co-operation can last. The time will come, however, when the gospel of Christ and the gospel of Marx will prescribe mutually opposed obligation, and that will be the time of testing. Either the Soviet Orthodox prelates must *de facto* give up their Christianity or ʙʀᴇᴀᴋ with the State and return to the previous period of fierce persecutions. The Russian Church is indeed the largest body of the Nonconformists in the Soviet Union, the most exposed and in the most delicate position.

THE NEW NONCONFORMISTS

Those Orthodox who reject any co-operation with the Soviet Government because it is godless form a special group which properly can be called the New Nonconformists. These Nonconformists undoubtedly exist in the Soviet Union itself, but they are disorganized and their significance cannot be evaluated. The organized opponents to the patriarch of Moscow reside abroad; and they form four distinct groups: the Russian Episcopal Synod Abroad, the Russian American Church, the Russian Exarchate of the Patriarchate of Constantinople for Western Europe, and the Ukrainian Autocephalous Church. The first three groups reject the absolute authority of the patriarch and allege that he is merely a tool of the godless Government which uses him to foster its political aims. Besides insisting on this same point, the Ukrainians claim that since they are a distinct nation they are entitled to have their own independent Church.

The Russian Episcopal Synod Abroad originated in the days of the Civil War when a temporary Supreme Ecclesiastical Administration of Southern Russia was created, with the consent of Patriarch Tychon, for the management of the affairs of dioceses occupied by the White Army. The administration was presided over by Anthony Khrapovitsky (1863–1936), metropolitan of Kiev, a pupil of Dostoevsky and admirer of Khomiakov.[19] In 1920 the last White Army left South Russia while about the same time another White Army retired abroad from Siberia, and a great many civilians left the country with the soldiers. The Supreme Administration, evacuated to Constantinople, moved in 1921 to Serbia and settled down in Sremski Karlovci, the residence of the patriarch of Serbia, and assumed the title of the Ecclesiastical Administration of the Russian Church Abroad.

During the same year the *émigrés* convened a Church Council in Sremski Karlovci, where, besides the prelates, both clergy and laity were represented. The council of the defeated exiles in due course condemned the victorious Soviet Government as godless and denounced Modernism, Freemasonry, and all organizations working against the Russian Church. The council also went on record as favoring the restoration of the house of Romanov in Russia.

The political resolutions of the council were opposed strongly by a large group led by Eulogius Georgievsky, archbishop of Volhynia, who considered such pronouncements dangerous and futile. Subsequent events demonstrated the futility of these declarations. The Bolsheviks used the Karlovci resolutions to the full in their persecution of the Russian Church and insinuated that most of the bishops were enemies of the Soviet regime and were plotting to overthrow it. The patriarch was obliged to act; and by a decree on April 22, 1922, the administration was dissolved and Archbishop Eulogius, who was made a metropolitan, was commissioned to take over its affairs. The new metropolitan failed, however, in his charge and allowed the dissolved administration to be revived under a new name — the Russian Episcopal Synod Abroad.[20]

The subsequent history of the Russian Church abroad is a long and bitter conflict between the episcopal synod, presided over first by Metropolitan Anthony and afterward by Metropolitan Anastasius, and its opponents in Europe and America. The synod derived its chief support from numerous Russian *émigrés* settled in the Balkans and in the Middle and Far East. This group stood for traditional Russian theology, a strong and centralized Church government, and the restoration of the imperial regime in a modified form. They distrusted the West and interdenominational movements and organizations. Most of them were rabidly anti-Bolshevik, and quite a few admired Hitler and Mussolini in their rise to power. Before World War II the synod resided in Serbia and was made up of the prelates who represented the four provinces into which the Church was divided — western Europe, the Balkans and the Middle East, the Far East, and America. In 1938 the synod directed about twenty dioceses and missions the world over and maintained a learned center through its faculty of theology at Harbin, Manchuria.[21] Metropolitan Anastasius, a strong anti-Bolshevik, looked for a time upon Hitler as a leader of mankind called to destroy Bolshevism; and he hoped that the German invasion of Russia in 1941 would result in the overthrow of the Soviet regime. During the war a good many prelates and clergy loyal to the episcopal synod collaborated with the Germans and were obliged to flee before the advancing Red armies. The synod itself moved first to Czechoslovakia and then to Munich in Bavaria, where it still resides. In 1945 the synod claimed to be recognized as the supreme authority by eighteen bishops, two hundred priests, and one million faithful, most of whom were Displaced Persons and *émigrés*.[22] As a consequence of the Soviet advance the synod lost its chief strongholds, the Balkans and the Far East. Its adherents at present are mostly Displaced Persons together with a few older *émigrés* in western Europe and in the Americas.

According to recent information the synod has eight bishops in North America: there are three dioceses and sixty-nine congregations. In South America there are four dioceses and several congregations. The synodal group has a seminary in the United States at Holy Trinity monastery, Jordanville, New York. Altogether the synod claims authority over 250 congregations the world over. (*Pravoslanaya Rus,* October 31, 1949.)

The synod's opponents in Europe, led by the late Metropolitan Eulogius, stood for an advance in theology along the way traced by Khomiakov and Soloviev. In politics they were more liberal and democratic. The spiritual center of this group was St. Sergius Theological Institute in Paris, which was founded in 1925. The late archpriest Sergius Bulgakov and Nicholas Berdyaev were the most remarkable men in the group, and both further developed Soloviev's daring speculations. The Paris group broke with the synod in 1926 and submitted to the late patriarch Sergius in 1927. It broke with Sergius in 1930, however, on a political issue and submitted to the patriarch of Constantinople, who claims jurisdiction over all the Orthodox in diaspora — although Russians generally do not admit his claims. The Paris group still is in the jurisdiction of Constantinople; and its head is Metropolitan Vladimir, who resides in Paris, the principal center for the group. While the followers of the synod technically are schismatics because their clergy are suspended by the Russian patriarch and consequently are not in communion with any other patriarch, the followers of Metropolitan Vladimir merely are excluded from the Russian Church and counted as members of the patriarchate of Constantinople, with which Moscow is in communion.[23]

The synodal opponents in America form their own autonomous province. The Russian Church in America dates from 1794, when the Russians established their missions in Alaska. In 1872 the Russians created a diocese in America for Orthodox immigrants from Europe. The Bolshevik Revolution separated this diocese from Moscow, and in 1921 Metropolitan Plato Rozhdestvensky assumed its direction. In 1926 he quarreled with the Russian Synod Abroad and left it; but after he died in 1934 his successor, Metropolitan Theophilus Pashkovsky, made peace with the synod. In 1940 the American Russian Church was a province with 330 parishes, divided into 6 dioceses with 400,000 faithful.[24] The Russian Americans again broke with the synod in 1946, and their efforts to achieve a complete independence from the Russian patriarchate by negotiation failed. Consequently the Russian American Church leads an independent existence. Their clergy are inhibited by Moscow, and from that point of view their position does not differ much from that of the synod, although neither the Americans nor the followers of the synod acknowledge their suspension. The American Russians now have a theological academy in New York City and a seminary in South Canaan, Pennsylvania. They have missionary dioceses in Japan, Alaska, and Argentina.

The Ukrainian Autocephalists date from 1921, when a Ukrainian nationalist clergyman, Archpriest Basil Lipkivsky, of Kiev, conceived the idea of separating the Ukrainian dioceses from the Russian patriarchate to organize them independently. Lipkivsky argued that the Ukrainian dioceses were transferred unjustly from the patriarchate of Constantinople to Moscow in 1686. If the Ukrainians are a distinct nation, Lipkivsky asserted, they are fully entitled to have their own Autocephalous Church; therefore he tried first to obtain the blessing of Patriarch Tychon in the setting up of such a Church. Undismayed by his failure to secure such a permission, the archpriest continued to work for the realization of his idea. In 1921, 400 of his followers met in Kiev and, proclaiming themselves the Ukrainian Church Council, enacted a resolution creating the Ukrainian Autocephalous Church with Lipkivsky as its primate. Since no Orthodox bishop would agree to consecrate Lipkivsky, who was a priest suspended by his patriarch, the Ukrainians decided to consecrate him by priests only. In following this course they invoked common Presbyterian arguments to justify their action. Lipkivsky was consecrated on October 23, 1921, by thirty priests in Kiev cathedral, where lay delegates, both men and women, joined in the ceremony of the laying on of hands.

Within a few days the new Ukrainian primate consecrated twenty-three bishops for the Ukrainians within the Soviet Union and abroad. Learning of Lipkivsky's acts, Patriarch Tychon excommunicated him and declared all his consecrations null and void. On March 25, 1922, he informed all other Orthodox patriarchs of his action and thus excluded the Autocephalists from the Orthodox Church. Excommunication, however, did not prevent Lipkivsky from continuing his activities. By 1924, 3,000 Ukrainian parishes out of 8,000 adhered to his Church. Like the Russian Renovators, Lipkivsky allowed married bishops and substituted the vernacular for the Church Slavonic in divine services. The Soviet authorities eagerly promoted Lipkivsky's activities for the same reason that they supported the Renovators — in order to discredit the Orthodox Church in the eyes of the masses. After the Autocephalists became influential and entered into relationships with the Ukrainian *émigrés* abroad, however, the Soviet authorities changed their policy. Lipkivsky and most of his principal assistants were imprisoned and within a few years his organization disintegrated.

The followers and sympathizers of Lipkivsky survived abroad, however, in Poland and in America. The Poles obtained vast provinces inhabited by four million Orthodox Ukrainians and White Russians, who were ecclesiastically under Moscow, after the Bolshevik defeat in 1920. The Polish Government detached these dioceses from the Russian Church against Patriarch Tychon's will and created out of them the Autocephalous Church of Poland, which was recognized by the patriarch of Constantinople. Many Ukrainians belonged to this Church and looked for the first opportunity to revive Lipkivsky's dreams. The collapse of Poland in 1939 afforded them that opportunity. An admirer of Lipkivsky, Polycarp Sikorsky, bishop of Lutsk in the Polish Church and a Ukrainian by race, received German support in reviving Lipkivsky's idea. Dionysius Valedinsky, the Polish primate, assisted Sikorsky, who, together with the late archbishop of Pinsv, Alexander Inosemtsev, revived in 1942 the Ukrainian Orthodox Autocephalous Church. These prelates consecrated bishops for the German occupied Ukrainian dioceses. The Orthodox canons, regulating episcopal consecrations, were often and intentionally disregarded. The patriarchate of Moscow, in whose jurisdiction Sikorsky had operated since 1939, excommunicated and unfrocked him and declared all his consecrations null and void. Sikorsky also met a strong resistance led by Metropolitan Alexis Gromadsky of Volynhia in the Ukraine itself. Although Gromadsky finally was assassinated by his enemies on May 7, 1943, the German collapse obliged Sikorsky and his bishops to flee from the Ukraine to Munich, where they now have their synod and theological faculty.[25]

The Autocephalists have at present, according to a reliable informant, 12 bishops and 400 clergy, who claim 150,000 followers in Europe and America. While their European faithful are mostly among the Displaced Persons, those in Canada and the United States are a prosperous community. The Autocephalists of America formed a diocese and elected as their prelate Archbishop John Teodorovich of Philadelphia, who was consecrated by Lipkivsky himself in 1921. Since no Orthodox group in America would recognize the consecration of Teodorovich as valid, he was very much isolated. According to *Ukrainska Zagalna Encyclopediya* (Lwów, 1937, Vol. III, page 926) Teodorovich's diocese included 152 congregations, of which 120 were in Canada.

In 1947 the Canadian Ukrainians formed their own diocese with the see in Winnipeg, where they have a flourishing institution for higher education, St. Andrew's College, which has a faculty of theology directed by Prof. D. Martinovsky. The present archbishop of Winnipeg is Mstislav Skrypnik, who belonged to the Sikorsky group. He is working to unite all the Ukrainians in the Americas into a single autonomous province under the jurisdiction of Constantinople.

The New Nonconformists are not really heretics in relationship to the Orthodox Church; they are not even true schismatics. They did not abandon the Russian patriarchate because it changed its rites or canons, and many of them may be considered simply as political opponents of the Soviet regime dressed in ecclesiastical garb. They protest against the godless Marxist philosophy of the Soviet state and against its methods and organization. They demand a full freedom of religion, democratic liberties, and social justice as they understand them. These New Nonconformists may be considered by many in the rest of Christendom as outdated in their beliefs and in their allegiances, but few will question their sincerity. As the fortunes of history change, these opponents of present-day native Russian Orthodoxy may yet exert an influence in the land of their origin.

THE OUTLOOK

I hope that I have presented a fair and reliable survey of Russian Nonconformity from its early beginnings to the present day. In the course of a very interesting discussion on "Prejudice in History" at Oxford some time ago, in which the eminent

Spanish historian, Salvador de Madariaga y Rojo, Canon Claude Jenkins, Regius Professor of Ecclesiastical History, and others, took part, a view was advanced that it is impossible to write an altogether impartial history. "*Pas d'histoire, seulement des histoires.*"

Among several scholars present neither de Madariaga nor Jenkins agreed with this view, propounded by skeptics. According to them a historian is like a painter making the picture of a hill. He paints what he sees from his point of view. If his presentation is correct, a good deal may be deducted about another side of the hill. Yet it may present quite a different picture. Canon Jenkins claimed that in order to be fair as a historian, it is often better to be an outsider having at the same time warm sympathy for and understanding of the people described, and he pointed out that one of the best histories of the Oxford Movement was written by a French Roman Catholic. If these are qualifications for the writing of history, I am justified in taking up the theme of Russian Nonconformity.

I am an outsider to Russian Nonconformity, born and bred in an Orthodox family; yet I have several ancestors who belonged to the "Old Faith." Indeed, my mother was trained in the Edinoverie ways; and I myself follow largely the Edinoverie usages. I have the utmost sympathy with and understanding of the Priestist Old Believers. I would be very sorry to misrepresent them; yet I would not foolishly idealize them as some people do. My father's ancestors belonged to the ancient Novgorodian stock, freedom-loving, adventurous, and freethinking. Consequently, I have a share in the Priestless inheritance, but while I admire much about them, I am less in sympathy with them than with the Priestists.

My mother's ancestors were from Nizhnii Novgorod on the Volga, the cradle of many Russian religious leaders, reformers, and statesmen such as Archpriests Avvakum and John Neronov, and Patriarchs Nikon and Sergius. My remote maternal ancestors came to Nizhni from Novgorod, deported by Ivan III when he destroyed the great Northern Republic. The Upper Volga was a classic home not only of the Raskol but also of several Russian sects. I knew the Molokans in my childhood; and later I met Russian Baptists, one of whom, Rev. Alexander Dobrynin, presented me with the Bible which I still use. I have had the opportunity to observe the life of the Russian Baptists for some time.

I have a few Ukrainian relations who were Uniate in the past, and Ukrainian history always has fascinated me. I also met and was a close friend of several eminent Russian Catholics and respected their point of view without sharing it. There is no doubt that the contribution of the Russian Catholics and the so-called Latinizers to Russian culture was always out of all proportion to their small number. Finally, I was in close contact with the leaders of the New Nonconformity. The late metropolitan Anthony Khrapovitsky, who resolutely opposed the policy of the late patriarch Sergius, was in a way my spiritual director for several years. I knew personally the late metropolitan Eulogius in Paris as well as a few leaders of the Ukrainian Autocephalists. Indeed, I have very good friends among them. Such widespread and yet close contacts with Russian Nonconformists of all shades have taught me to understand a good deal about the Russian Nonconformists and to feel a great sympathy toward them. I have remained, nevertheless, unshakably loyal to the Russian Orthodox Church as represented by the patriarchate of Moscow. Neither my parents nor my relatives were overenthusiastic about the synodal regime, although some of them benefited by it — indeed one of them was the Russian primate of the imperial age — but they were loyal to the Church.

Hoping that my presentation of Russian Nonconformity has been fair enough, I venture to express my view as to its future. The first Russian Nonconformists, the Strigolniks, their successors the Judaizers, and afterward the Nonpossessors, fought for freedom of conscience. The Raskolniks struggled against the State's enforcing upon them ecclesiastical reforms which they did not want. The Ukrainian Cossacks fought the Poles not only for the same reasons as the Raskolniks did but also for their national culture and independence. The Uniates resisted the Poles and then the Russians, for the same reasons. The New Nonconformists resist the Russian patriarchate primarily for political reasons, for they believe the patriarchate is merely a Soviet tool.

Yet the Russian Church itself is no longer the established religion but merely the largest Nonconformist body in the Soviet Union, where Marxist-Leninism is a dominant faith. This new creed is, according to Lenin, fundamentally hostile to any religion, being based on the dialectical materialism of Karl Marx, itself derived from French atheism of the eighteenth century and from Feuerbach. (Lenin, in *Sochineniia*, Vol. XIV, page 68.) Stalin shares, naturally, a similar view as is so often pointed out by the Soviet writers; but up to a point he disliked the violent persecution of religion. According to Lenin and Stalin, religion will die a natural death in the Communist society when the class foundations of religion are destroyed and the scientific outlook supersedes religious beliefs. So far this has not happened. Bolshevism itself has become a religion far more intolerant than Orthodoxy, which never pretended to control science as Bolshevism does. Today Russian biologists, physicists, astronomers, and other scientists must adhere to Marxian dialectics as to revealed dogma. Anything that contradicts Marxism is declared false and unscientific, however acceptable it may be to scientists. Such a conflict of Marxism with science cannot last forever. In the end the former must give up its claim to be " Scientific Socialism " and remain what, strictly speaking, it is, an outdated and old-fashioned philosophical and economic system. There is, however, every prospect that Marxian dogma will be revised in due course to suit new conditions. Its violent atheism may be dropped.

Christianity has survived Islam, the great Bogomil heresy, the storm and stress giving rise to the Renaissance and Reformation, the eighteenth century Enlightenment and the French Revolution, as well as the radicalism and agnosticism of the nineteenth century. It will survive the Communist era as well. Mighty is the truth, and it prevails! No believing Christian need be afraid for the future of Christianity, least of all for Christianity in Russia. The Russian Church survived the fiery storm of the Bolshevik Revolution and emerged stronger and purer. All the unreliable elements, all the unconverted people — the camp followers and those for whom the Church was merely a useful social institution — left the Church. Only those convinced of the divine truth of the gospel remained. No doubt the Russian Church, being now the largest Nonconformist body in the Soviet Union, is in a delicate position. There is no guarantee that violent persecution will not begin anew, for the deep-seated conflict between Christianity and Marxism can never be solved and may always flare up. Only when Communism gives up its present philosophical basis and ceases to be Marxian will its fundamental opposition to Christianity end.

Christianity's position in the Soviet Union is not unlike that of Christianity in the Islamic countries. Like Bolshevism, early Islam was an intolerant, aggressive, and missionary creed. Like a tornado it swept the vast expanses of Asia, Africa, and Europe, preaching its creed by sword and fire. Although Islam succeeded in destroying altogether some Christian communities in Asia and Africa, mostly superficially Christianized and rent by divisions, it could not uproot Christianity where it was firmly established. In the end a *modus vivendi* was found, and the two religions were forced to exist side by side. Gradually, Islam began to retreat and not only lost its dynamic character but became a burden and an obstacle to the progress of nations which adopted it. It is doubtful that Bolshevism is stronger than Islam; far more likely that it is weaker.

The Communists already have realized that they cannot exterminate Christianity in Russia. It has existed there for a thousand years; and all Russian culture and history are so closely connected with Christianity that they cannot be taught to children and assimilated by adults without a knowledge and understanding of what Christianity is. In a great multitude of Russian novelists, artists, musicians, historians, and scholars of the past Christ has his own missionaries who cannot be silenced. They preach indeed exceedingly well, and even today the clergy hardly have the time and strength to prepare for final admission the enthusiastic converts to the Church.

Although difficulties facing the Russian Church are great, they are less than those in the West where skepticism and religious indifferentism are so strongly entrenched. The latter are far more difficult to overcome than an open hostility. It is a well-known fact that the best way to enfeeble Christianity is to make it an Established Church and to load its upper clergy with all kinds of honor, power, and wealth. These things indeed are dangerous and corrupting. The history of the late Middle Ages, of pre-Revolutionary France, and of imperial Russia provide good illustrations. Fr. Benson, founder of the Anglican Religious Society of St. John the Evangelist in Oxford, was perfectly right when he said to his disciples: " Be cheerful, when the world despises, ridicules, and persecutes you — they did so to Christ — but be uneasy and watchful when people start to admire you and load you with honors and gifts."

It is always dangerous to prophesy, still trends and circumstances in the Soviet Union point to the growing and deepening revival of Christianity in Russia, particularly among the Orthodox and the Protestants. Like Orthodoxy, Protestantism represents a long and well-established tradition in the country. The Protestant groups are native and independent, dynamic and adaptable. Long years of persecution have taught them to unite their forces and to avoid the internal struggles which have plagued Protestantism for so long. The Russian Protestants have not only a good chance to survive but they may be expected to develop and to organize themselves into a serious spiritual force.

The Raskol and Russian Catholicism are in a more difficult position. The first is too negative in its doctrine, too attached to a definite period in the Russian history which it highly idealizes. Life has changed so much that the controversies and dominant ideas of Muscovy in the seventeenth century have become now altogether meaningless. The Raskol opposed the Russian Orthodox Church, reformed by Nikon and by Peter the Great, because it was the Established Church, dominated by the ungodly government, which persecuted the Raskolniks. Now the Russian Church itself is merely the largest Nonconformist body, and it has become pointless to oppose the Church in the same way as in the past. The Raskol can, of course, continue to oppose the Soviet power as satanic just as it opposed the imperial power in the past; but such a position can scarcely encourage vigor and growth.

It is not merely a coincidence that the Priestists, who are nearest in the Raskol to the Church, have survived well; while the radical, irreconcilable Priestless have become reduced to an insignificant group.

The Russian Catholics face the greatest difficulties of all in the Soviet Union. Apart from a few isolated Great Russians and some White Russians, these Catholics are nearly all the Ukrainian Uniates of Galicia, Bukovina, and sub-Carpathian Russia. Powerful political reasons urge the Soviet Government to destroy them. The Uniates, by tradition, look to the West. Since the last century they have become the advance guard of Ukrainian nationalism, which aims to separate the Ukrainian lands from the control of Moscow and to set up an independent and, by force of events, a hostile state to the Great Russians. It is a Macedonian, Irish, and Catalonian question rolled into one but in a far more formidable form.

Moscow faced the same problem in the fifteenth century with Novgorod and solved it by ending the ecclesiastical autonomy of Novgorod, by dispersing anti-Muscovites, and by exchanging populations on a vast scale. The Muscovites succeeded very well because the rank and file of the Novgorodians were indifferent to their own nationalists and cared little about their ecclesiastical autonomy. The Russian empire failed to eliminate the Raskolniks and the Russian Protestants, while it succeeded in suppressing the Uniates in the nineteenth century. Why? Because the Uniate rank and file cared little about their connection with Rome and positively disliked or even hated the Latin Catholics, whom they identified with their Polish or Hungarian landlords.

The vast movement from Uniatism to Orthodoxy, which has taken place in the last fifty years among the Galician and sub-Carpathian Uniate immigrants in the United States and Canada, as well as among the Uniates of Czechoslovakia, has revealed that the Union with Rome is still unimportant to many ordinary Uniates. Although there were many people who willingly joined the Russian Church in Galicia in 1946, there were no doubt also many opponents. Given time, the Soviet Government probably will reduce them by judicial exchange of populations and by other means. In the past the Union never had a great grip on the Ukrainian or White Russian masses. Within a couple of generations hardly any trace remained of it in Volhynia, Podolia, and White Russia, where the imperial Government abolished the Union in the nineteenth century and earlier. If, however, prospects for the Uniates under the Soviet Government are not rosy, they have the fullest chance to develop in the United States, Canada, and South America. The Russian Catholics proper hardly ever will be numerous but they always will attract a certain number of highly gifted people through whom they will exercise an influence out of all proportion to their number.

Russian "New Nonconformity" is in large part a political opposition to the Soviet regime dressed in an ecclesiastical garb. The New Nonconformists oppose the Russian patriarchate not because it changed the doctrine, rites, or canons of the Church but because it co-operates with the godless Government. According to the opposition, the patriarchate in identifying itself with the Soviet regime became its tool and agency and, therefore, must be opposed. This New Nonconformity is unlikely to continue for long as a significant movement outside of Russia. New generations lose contact with the old country, its traditions, prejudices, and fancies; and the struggles and conflicts of the Old World mean little to them. The Russian Orthodox in America together with the descendants of the Greek, Rumanian, Serb, Bulgarian, Syrian, and other Orthodox immigrants may form in due course, perhaps within a couple of generations, an English-speaking Autocephalous Orthodox American Church of some millions strong. All present difficulties facing the Orthodox in America are those of transition. Those Russian exiles and Displaced Persons who live in Europe, Asia, and Australia, where the Orthodox are few and far between, either will disappear in due course as they are absorbed into the native population and adopt its religion; or they will return in their allegiance to the patriarchate when circumstances change. These Nonconformist groups abroad are interesting, but they do not promise to live long. Their chief importance lies in the fact that they make Orthodoxy known abroad, promoting thereby the *rapprochement* between the East and the West.

Within the Soviet Union itself, however, the New Nonconformists — discontented Orthodox, Protestants, and Uniates who object to their superiors because they co-operate with the Government — go " underground " just as older Nonconformists did in the past. No one knows the size or the strength of this religious underground in Russia today, but the fact that it does exist and that it will someday come to the surface and make its influence felt can scarcely be doubted. A Croatian Roman Catholic priest, writing under the pseudonym Father George, describes in a recent popular book entitled *God's Underground*[1] a visit of several months in Soviet Russia during which he came into contact with a large number of secretly organized Christian groups. The story that he tells with the literary assistance of Gretta Palmer is a startling account of religious activity involving not only devout peasants and workers but also high Government and military officials. While this story is not capable of objective proof, the history of Russian Nonconformity, with its amazing continuity through underground activity, lends credibility to the basic claims of the author. Prof. Matthew Spinka in reviewing the book has expressed doubts concerning the authenticity of some of the things that it reports. Nevertheless he concludes: " Undoubtedly there is a basis of fact in what he tells us of the status of religion within the Soviet Union, and it is this residuum of factual information which is highly important. I wish it were all true." [2]

On the whole, the outlook for Russian Nonconformity is a good one. The Nonconformists will continue to preach Christ as they have done before and to preserve the tradition of independence and zeal for their convictions which will make its mark both on the Russian Church and on the Russian State.

NOTES

INTRODUCTION

[1] P. Melnikov studied the problem of the exact number of the Non-conformists in Russia in his essay "Schislenie raskolnikov," *Sochineniia*, Marks, St. Petersburg, 1909, Vol. VII, pp. 384–409.

[2] *Ibid.*, p. 400.

[3] *Ibid.*, p. 392.

[4] *Ibid.*, p. 400.

[5] *Ibid.*, p. 405.

[6] *Ibid.*, p. 400.

[7] *Ibid.*, p. 203.

[8] P. Miliukov, *Outlines of Russian Culture*, University of Pennsylvania Press, 1942, Vol. I, p. 116.

[9] *Ibid.*, p. 119.

CHAPTER I

[1] An interesting view on Russian conversion is expressed by N. Baumgarten in his "St. Vladimir et la conversion de la Russie," *Orientalia Christiana*, 79, Rome, 1932.

[2] B. Leib in his *Rome, Kiev et Byzance à la fin du XI siècle (1088–1099)*, Picard, Paris, 1924, gives a good picture of the period. Also consult F. Dvornik, *The Making of Central and Eastern Europe*, The Polish Research Centre, London, 1949.

[3] L. Goetz, in *Das Kiever Höhlenkloster als Kulturzentrum der vormongolischen Zeit*, M. Waldbauer, Passau, 1904, stresses well the importance of Lavra for Russia.

[4] J. Hammer-Purgstall, *Geschichte der Goldenen Horde im Kiptschak*, Hartleben, Pesth, 1840, is one of the best works on Mongols in Russia. Another good study is D'Osson, *Istoriia mongolov*, Irkutsk, 1937.

[5] There is an English translation of S. Borodin's *Dimitri Donskoy*, published first by Ogis, Kuibyshev, 1942.

CHAPTER II

[1] On the background of the Strigolniks and on the clergy of Pskov consult I. Beliaev, *Istoriia goroda Pskova i Pskovskoi zemli*, Synodal Printing Press, Moscow, 1867, pp. 63–94.

[2] There are two good essays on the Judaizers: one by N. Panov, "Eres

Zhidovstvuiustchikh," *Zhurnal Ministerstva Narodnago Prosvestcheniia,* St. Petersburg, 1877–1878; and another by Servitsky, " Opyt Izsledovaniia Eresi Zhidovstvuiustchikh," *Pravoslavnoe Obozrenie,* 1862.

CHAPTER III

[1] Dr. N. Zernov's *Moscow the Third Rome,* S. P. C. K., London, 1937, studies the period. There is a good article in French on the leaders of the Josephites and the Nonpossessors in *Irénikon,* T. XIV, NN 4–5, 1937 (Amay, Belgium), by Mme. Behr-Sigel, " Nil Sorsky et Joseph de Volo-kolamsk."

[2] Printed in Kazan in 1857; a good edition.

[3] Dr. N. Zernov's *St. Sergius, Builder of Russia,* S. P. C. K., London, 1937, is a good study.

[4] Philaret, archbishop of Kharkov, *Obzor russkoi Dukhovnoi literatury,* Kharkov University Press, Kharkov, 1859, Vol. I, pp. 167, 168.

[5] Nil Sorsky's *Tvoreniia (Writings)* was published in St. Petersburg in 1864.

CHAPTER IV

[1] E. Denisoff published in Paris in 1942 a remarkable study of Maximus' early years, *Maxime le Grec et l'Occident.* Maximus' life and works are described by Ikonnikov in Russian, *Maksim Grek i ego vremia,* Kiev, 1915. Maximus, although not formally canonized, is looked upon as a saint.

[2] The best book on Avvakum and the beginning of the Raskol in a western European language is that by P. Pascal, *Avvakum et les débuts du Raskol,* Istina, Paris, 1938. It has an exhaustive bibliography.

[3] The greatest study of the patriarch Nikon in English is by W. Palmer, *The Patriarch Nikon,* Trübner, London, 1871–1876, 6 vols.

CHAPTER V

[1] E. Shleev, "Pravoslavnoe Staroobriadchestvo," *Zhurnal Moskovskoi Patriarkhii,* Moscow, July, 1946, p. 29.

[2] The summary of "Okruzhnoe Poslanie" can be found in *Pravoslavnaia Bogoslovskaia Entsiklopediia,* Vol. II, cols. 1264–1265.

[3] V. Ryabushinsky, *Staroobriadchestvo i russkoe religioznoe chuvstvo,* Private Edition, Joinville-le-Pont, 1936, p. 90.

[4] J. K. Buikovsky, *Istoriia Staroobriadchestva vsekh soglasii,* Filatov Printers, Moscow, 1906, pp. 66–67.

[5] *Zhurnal Moskovskoi Patriarkhii,* July, 1946, pp. 31–34.

[6] According to the last volume: *S. S. S. R., Bolshaia Sovetskaia Entsiklopediia,* Moscow, 1947, col. 1787, there exists still a group of the Priest-ists, who do not adhere to Bela Krynitsa but obtain their clergy from the Orthodox Church. These Beglopopovtsy have as their head Archbishop John, who is sixty-three years old. The Beglopopovtsy still recruit their clergy from the deserters from the Russian Church.

CHAPTER VI

[1] P. Miliukov, *op. cit.,* p. 59.

[2] V. Anderson, *Staroobriadchestvo i sektantstvo,* V. Gubinsky, St.

Petersburg, 1909, p. 132. The best history of Vyg is by Filippov, *Istoriia Vygovskoi staroobriadcheskoi pustyni*, Moscow, 1862.

[3] Anderson, *op. cit.*, pp. 134, 135.

[4] *Russkii Entsiklopedicheskii Slovar'*, Book 7, pp. 486–487.

[5] Anderson, *op. cit.*, p. 144.

[6] V. Andreev, *Raskol i ego znachenie v narodnoi russkoi istorii*, M. Khan's Printing Press, St. Petersburg, 1870, pp. 150, 151.

[7] Anderson, *op. cit.*, p. 165.

[8] *Pravoslavnaia Bogoslovskaia Entsiklopediia*, II, col. 324.

[9] The best monograph on the Wanderers is by Prof. N. Ivanovsky, *Vnutrennee Ustroistvo sekty Strannikov ili Begunov*, Missionerskoe Obozrenie, St. Petersburg, 1901.

[10] Dobroklonsky, *Rukovodstvo po istorii Russkoi Tserkvi*, Moscow University Press, 1893, IV, p. 378.

[11] From Rev. S. Evans' address to St. John Damascene Society on November 16, 1946, *Irénikon*, T. XX, pp. 213–214.

[12] I. Yuzov, *Starovery i Dukhovnye Khristiane*, St. Petersburg, 1881, p. 46.

[13] According to S. S. S. R., *Bolshaia Sovetskaia Entsiklopediia*, Moscow, 1947, col. 1790, the Priestless have in Moscow the Supreme Spiritual Council, which supervises their congregations.

Chapter VII

[1] See "Ukaz Sinoda," August 7, 1734, in *Polnoe sobranie zakonov rossiiskoi imperii*, T. IX, No. 6613.

[2] C. Kutepov, *Sekty Khlystov i Skoptsov*, T. Timofeev's Printing Press, Stavropol, 1900, p. 38. Melnikov thinks, however, that the Khlysty existed already in the reign of Ivan the Terrible, *Sochineniia*, Marks, St. Petersburg, 1909, Vol. VI, pp. 251 ff.

[3] Reutsky, *Liudi Bozhii i Skoptsy*, Grachev Printers, Moscow, 1872, p. 42.

[4] Kutepov, *op. cit.*, pp. 83, 84.

[5] V. Bonch-Bruevich, *Materialy k istorii i izucheniiu russkago sektantstva i raskola*.

[6] The seventh volume of Bonch-Bruevich's *Materialy* is dedicated to the Old Israel.

[7] One of the most revealing books on Rasputin is by Fülöp-Miller, *Rasputin, the Holy Devil*, Putnam, London, 1928.

[8] *Bolshaia Sovetskaia Entsiklopediia*, Vol. 29, p. 75.

[9] Dobroklonsky, *op. cit.*, pp. 342–344; Kutepov, *op. cit.*, pp. 260–291.

[10] Kutepov, *op. cit.*, pp. 292–306.

[11] Sometimes the Khlysty use the Indian songs, much disfigured Sanscrit hymns. See Melnikov, *op. cit.*, Vol. V, p. 95.

[12] Who was the founder of the Skoptsy is still unknown. Reutsky believed him to be a certain Khlyst Andrew Petrov; Nadezhdin, Dmitrievsky, and others believed him to be an Orel peasant Conrad or Andrew Selivanov. See Kutepov, *op. cit.*, pp. 107–109.

[13] Quoted in full by Anderson, *op. cit.*, pp. 325–339.

[14] P. Melnikov, *op. cit.*, p. 408.

[15] There is a good biography of Mrs. Tatarinov in *Russkii Biograficheskii Slovar'*, Vol. 20, pp. 316–320, with a large bibliography. Mrs. Tatarinov's dossier is in the archives of the high procurator of the Most Holy Synod, case 54.

CHAPTER VIII

[1] Anderson, *op. cit.*, p. 373; Andreev, *op. cit.*, p. 245.

[2] A good short biography of Tveritinov can be found in *Russkii Biograficheskii Slovar'*, Vol. 20, pp. 381–385.

[3] See details in Longinov, *Novikov i Moskovskie Martinisty*, Moscow, 1867; also, V. Bogoliubov, *Novikov i ego vremiia*, Moscow, 1916.

[4] Born in a noble family Labzin was educated in Moscow University and became a Freemason in 1783. He founded his own brand of Free-masonry in 1800. Labzin's religious views were very nearly those of the Quakers. He was a voluminous writer and translator. Details: *Russkii Biograficheskii Slovar'*, Vol. 10, pp. 2–12.

[5] J. F. C. Wright, *Slava Bohu, The Story of the Dukhobors*, Farrar & Rinehart, Inc., New York, 1940, pp. 42–46.

[6] Dobroklonsky, *op. cit.*, IV, pp. 370, 371; Anderson, *op. cit.*, pp. 395–409.

[7] Wright, *op. cit.*, p. 437.

[8] According to Miliukov, *op. cit.*, p. 114, "During 1920, almost fifteen thousand Dukhobors, who had remained in Russia, together with the Molokans were transferred from the Caucasus to Salsk, a district which had belonged previously to the Cossacks."

[9] V. Bonch-Bruevich published the Dukhobor Psalter of "Zhivotnaia kniga" in the second volume of his *Materialy*.

[10] Dobroklonsky, *op. cit.*, IV, pp. 355–356.

[11] From the Dukhobor "Ispovedanie," quoted by Anderson, *op. cit.*, p. 377.

[12] N. Nikolsky, *Istoriia Russkoi Tserkvi*, Atheist, Moscow, 1930, p. 206.

[13] *Russkii Entsiklopedicheskii Slovar'*, XI, 944.

[14] *Ibid.*, XIII, 769.

[15] *The Jewish Encyclopedia*, New York, 1925, Vol. III, p. 630.

[16] Anderson, *op. cit.*, p. 417.

[17] Dobroklonsky, *op. cit.*, IV, p. 365.

[18] V. Yasevich-Borodaevskaia, *Borba za veru*, State Printing Press, St. Petersburg, 1912, pp. 250–277.

[19] Dobroklonsky, *op. cit.*, IV, p. 362.

[20] According to S. S. S. R., *Bolshaia Sovetskaia Entsiklopediia*, Moscow, 1947, the independent Molokans still exist in the Soviet Union. The majority, however, fused with the Baptists.

[21] Anderson, *op. cit.*, pp. 419, 420.

[22] Nikolsky, *op. cit.*, p. 246.

CHAPTER IX

[1] J. H. Rushbrooke, *The Baptist Movement on the Continent of Europe*, Carey Press, London, 1923, p. 133.

[2] See Ushinsky, *Verouchenie Malorusskikh Shtundistov*, Kiev, 1886; also, T. Melnikov, *O Sektantskom Sviastchenstve*, Voskresnoe Chtenie, Warsaw, 1933–1934.

[3] J. H. Rushbrooke, *Some Chapters of European Baptist History*, Kingsgate Press, London, 1929, pp. 87, 88.

[4] V. Bonch-Bruevich, *Materialy k istorii i izucheniiu russkago sektantstva i raskola*, St. Petersburg, 1908, Vol. I, p. 1.

[5] Rushbrooke, *Some Chapters*, p. 95.

[6] On Uvarov's nationalism see Dr. L. Strakhovsky, *L'Empereur Nicholas Ier et l'esprit national russe*, Librairie Universitaire, Louvain, 1928.

[7] J. Hecker, *Religion and Communism*, Chapman, London, 1933, p. 78.

[8] Details on the Soviet encouragement of the Baptists and the Evangelicals may be read in T. Melnikov, *Sektantstvo i Tserkov*, Kishinev, 1934.

[9] Rushbrooke, *The Baptist Movement*, p. 138.

[10] Rushbrooke, *Some Chapters*, p. 103.

[11] *Soviet War News*, August 22, 1941, quoted by S. Bolshakoff, *The Christian Church and the Soviet State*, S. P. C. K., London, 1942, pp. 59, 60.

[12] Based on communication of P. L. Meacham.

[13] *The Church in the World*, March, 1946.

[14] Quoted from *Religion and the People*, Birmingham, April, 1947.

[15] *Bratskii Vestnik*, Moscow, January, 1948.

[16] Details in J. Chistovich, *Istoriia perevoda Biblii na russkii yazyk*, Khristianskoe Chtenie, St. Petersburg, 1872–1873.

[17] A good description of Count Protasov, Metropolitan Philaret Drozdov, and Russian clergy in the forties of the last century is given by W. Palmer in his *Notes of a Visit to the Russian Church*, Kegan Paul, London, 1882.

CHAPTER X

[1] See for details, Metropolitan Macarius Bulgakov, *Istoriia Russkoi Tserkvi*, Golicke and Wilborg, St. Petersburg, 1883–1903, Vol. IX.

[2] *Ibid.*, pp. 321–323.

[3] *Ibid.*, pp. 618–635. The metropolitan thinks that while other Ruthenian prelates could act for unworthy motives Pociej did so for conviction.

[4] D. Doroshenko, *History of the Ukraine*, Ukrainian Self-reliance League of Canada, Edmonton, Canada, 1939, pp. 134, 135.

[5] Metropolitan Peter Mohyla, *Confession of Orthodox Faith*, T. Baker, London, 1898.

[6] See details in Koialovich, *Istoriia Vozsoedineniia Zapadno-Russkich Uniatov Starykh Vremen*, St. Petersburg, 1872.

[7] A. P. Lopukhin, *Istoriia Khristianskoi Tserkvi v XIX veke*, St. Petersburg, 1901, Vol. II, pp. 600–603.

[8] M. Derrick, *Eastern Catholics Under Soviet Rule*, Sword of the Spirit, London, 1946, p. 16.

[9] Lopukhin, *op. cit.*, Vol. I, p. 134.

[10] *Zhurnal Moskovskoi Patriarkhii*, April, 1946, p. 35.

[11] *The Christian East*, London, April, 1935, p. 23.

[12] Prozorovsky wrote a good monograph, *Silvestr Medvedev*, Chteniya, Moscow, 1896.

[13] P. H. Lemcke's *Life and Work of Prince Demetrius Augustine Gallitzine*, Longmans, Green & Co., Inc., New York, 1940, is still the best.

[14] M. J. Rouet de Journel, S. J., *Un Collège de Jesuites à St. Petersbourg*, Perrin, Paris, 1922, p. 78.

[15] M. J. Rouet de Journel, S. J., *Madame Swetchine*, Boone Presse, Paris, 1929, p. 158.

[16] Prince Ivan Gagarin, S. J., was the author of *La Russie sera-t-elle catholique?* Douniol, Paris, 1856.

[17] Canon Charles Quenet published an excellent study *Tchaadaev et les lettres philosophiques*, Champion, Paris, 1931.

[18] Gershenson wrote a curious book *Vladimir Pecherin*, Istoriia Molodoi Rossii, Moscow, 1932.

[19] The English translation of the famous V. Soloviev's work *Russia and the Universal Church* was published in London in 1948 by Geoffrey Bles, Ltd.

[20] The best summary of Soloviev's teaching, approved by the philosopher himself, was given by P. Miliukov, *Iz istorii russkoy intilligentsii*, Znanie, St. Petersburg, 1902, pp. 296–298.

[21] V. Soloviev, *Istoriia i budushchnost teokratii*, Zagreb, 1887, p. 22.

[22] The best study on Soloviev is by C. Mochulsky, *V. Soloviev*, Y. M. C. A. Press, Paris, 1937. D. Stremoukhov's *Vladimir Soloviev et son œuvre messianique*, Les Belles Lettres, Paris, 1935, is good. M. d'Herbigny's *A Russian Newman*, London, 1918, is outdated.

[23] For details see P. Volkonsky's "A Brief Sketch of the Organization of the Russian Catholic Church in Russia," published from February until July, 1941, in *Voice of the Church*, St. Procopius Abbey, Lisle, Illinois, U. S. A.

CHAPTER XI

[1] There is a good life of Prokopovich by Prof. B. Titlinov in *Russkii Biograficheskii Slovar'*, St. Petersburg, 1896–1918, Vol. XXV, pp. 399–448. John Chistovich's *Feofan Prokopovich i ego vremia*, St. Petersburg, 1868, is a good monograph.

[2] G. Samarin in his *Stefan Yavorsky i Feofan Prokopovich*, Moscow, 1880, gives a good appraisal of both.

[3] See A. Molchanovsky, "Dva proekta vosstanovleniia patriarchestva v Rossii v XVIII veke," *Zhurnal Moskovskoi Patriarkhii*, December, 1944, pp. 52–58.

[4] For details see his life by Ikonnikov, *Arsenii Matseievich*, Russkaya Starina, 1879, Vols. 24–26.

[5] See on Khomiakov, S. Bolshakoff, *The Doctrine of the Unity of the Church in the Works of Khomyakov and Moehler*, S.P.C.K., London, 1946.

[6] J. Curtiss in his *State and Church in Russia, 1901–1917*, Columbia University Press, New York, 1940, describes the period in great detail.

[7] Lopukhin, *Istoriia*, Vol. II, p. 695.

[8] See A. Dobroklonsky, *Rukovodstvo po istorii Russkoi Tserkvi*, Moscow University Press, 1893, Vol. 4.

⁹ J. Hecker, *Religion and Communism,* Chapman & Hall, New York, 1934; London, 1933, pp. 224–226.

¹⁰ P. Miliukov, *op. cit.,* p. 156. Mitropolit Evlogii Georgievsky, *Put' moei zhizni,* Y.M.C.A. Press, Paris, 1947, p. 301.

¹¹ See details in M. Spinka, *The Church and the Russian Revolution,* The Macmillan Company, New York, 1927, Chapters V and VI.

¹² S. Bolshakoff, *The Christian Church and the Soviet State,* S.P.C.K., London, 1942, pp. 36–37.

¹³ P. B. Anderson, *People, Church and State in Modern Russia,* S.C.M. Press, 1944, p. 64. P. Miliukov, *op. cit.,* p. 205.

¹⁴ See *Zhurnal Moskovskoi Patriarkhii,* NN 1, 4, and 10, 1944.

¹⁵ P. B. Anderson gives a good summary of the period in his book, Chapters VI and VII, pp. 77–120.

¹⁶ Bolshakoff, *The Christian Church and the Soviet State,* p. 43.

¹⁷ See details in Phillips Price, *Russia, Red or White, A Record of a Visit to Russia After 27 Years,* Low, London, 1948.

¹⁸ Quoted from *The Tablet,* London, June 19, 1948.

¹⁹ See his life in S. Bolshakoff, " Le Metropolite Antoine de Kiev," *Irénikon,* Amay, September–October, 1936.

²⁰ Consult M. d'Herbigny and A. Deubner, *Evêques russes en exil,* Orientalia Christiana, Rome, 1931.

²¹ S. Bolshakoff, *The Foreign Missions of the Russian Orthodox Church,* S.P.C.K., London, 1943, p. 110.

²² *Letopis,* Lausanne, 1945, p. 17.

²³ A very detailed description of that group is found in Mitropolit Evlogii Georgievsky's book referred to above.

²⁴ According to Bishop Leontius of Chicago, article in *Khleb Nebesnyi,* Harbin, July, 1940.

²⁵ The best short study of the Autocephalists is by S. Raevsky, *Ukrainskaia Avtokefalnaia Tserkov,* Jordanville, New York, 1948.

THE OUTLOOK

¹ *God's Underground,* by Father George as told to Gretta Palmer, Appleton-Century-Crofts, Inc., 1949.

² *The Westminster Bookman,* IX, 1, September–October, 1949.

SELECT BIBLIOGRAPHY

(NOTE: Only the most important sources or readily available books are included here. Most of the volumes listed in this bibliography can be found in American libraries. A vast and specialized literature on the subject is available for students. Several books included in the list contain extensive bibliographies.)

Anderson, P. B., *People, Church and State in Modern Russia,* The Macmillan Company, 1944.
Anderson, V., *Staroobriadchestvo i sektantstvo,* Gubinsky, St. Petersburg, 1909. Valuable.
Andreev, V., *Raskol i ego znachenie v narodnoi russkoi istorii,* M. Khan's Printing Press, St. Petersburg, 1870. Very original.
Andrusyak, N., *Église Ruthène, Dictionnaire de Théologie Catholique,* Vol. CXXV–CXXVI, Paris, 1938.
Arkhangelsky, A. S., *Nil Sorsky i Vassian Patrikeev, ikh literaturnye trudy i idei v drevney Rusi,* Pamyatniki Drevney Pismennosti, St. Petersburg, 1882.
Arseniev, N., *Holy Moscow,* S. P. C. K., London, 1940.
Avvakum, Archpriest, *Life,* London, 1926.

Beliaev, I., *Razskazy iz russkoi istorii,* Synodal Printing Press, Moscow, 1866–1872, 4 vols.
——, *Istoriia Novgoroda Velikago,* Synodal Printing Press, Moscow, 1866.
——, *Istoriia goroda Pskova i Pskovskoi zemli,* Synodal Printing Press, Moscow, 1867.
Berdyaev, N., *A. S. Khomiakov,* Put', Moscow, 1912.
Biriukov, P., *Dukhobortsy,* Posrednik, St. Petersburg, 1912.
Bolshaia Sovetskaia Entsiklopediia, Moscow, not completed.
Bolshakoff, S., "Le Metropolite Antoine de Kiev," *Irénikon,* Amay, September–October, 1936.

——, *The Christian Church and the Soviet State,* The Macmillan Company, 1942.

——, *The Foreign Missions of the Russian Orthodox Church,* S. P. C. K., London, 1943.

——, " Christian Unity, Personal Study of a Great Problem," *Voice of the Church,* St. Procopius Abbey, Lisle, Illinois, U.S.A., from 1941 to 1944. Discusses conflicts among Russian churchmen abroad.

——, *The Doctrine of the Unity of the Church in the Works of Khomyakov and Moehler,* S. P. C. K., London, 1946.

Bonch-Bruevich, V., *Materialy k istorii i izucheniiu russkago sektantstva i raskola,* St. Petersburg, 1908–1916, 7 vols. A good collection of documents.

Buikovsky, J. K., *Istoriia Staroobriadchestva vsekh soglasii,* Filatov Printers, Moscow, 1906. Curious.

Bulgakov, Metropolitan Macarius, *Istoriia Russkoi Tserkvi,* Golicke and Wilborg, St. Petersburg, 1883–1903, 12 vols. Good bibliography and documents.

Bulgakov, S., *The Wisdom of God,* Williams and Norgate, London, 1937.

——, *The Orthodox Church,* Centenary Press, London, 1938.

Chodynicki, K., *Kosciol Prawoslawny a Rzeczpospolita Polska (1370–1632),* Warsaw, 1934.

Curtiss, J., *State and Church in Russia, 1901–1917,* Columbia University Press, New York, 1940.

Danzas, J., *The Russian Church,* Sheed & Ward, Inc., London, 1936. Popular.

Denisov, S., *Vinograd rossiiskii,* Moscow, 1906. Sources.

Derrick, M., *Eastern Catholics Under Soviet Rule,* Sword of the Spirit, London, 1946.

d'Herbigny, M., *L'Église Orthodoxe Panukrainienne, documents inédits,* Collected by M. d'Herbigny, S.J., *Orientalia Christiana,* Rome, 1923, issues 3 and 4.

Dobroklonsky, A., *Rukovodstvo po istorii Russkoi Tserkvi,* Moscow University Press, 1893, 4 vols. A very extensive bibliography.

Doroshenko, D., *History of the Ukraine,* Ukrainian Self-reliance League of Canada, Edmonton, Canada, 1939.

Dvornik, F., *Les Slavs, Byzance et Rome au IXe siècle,* Champion, Paris, 1926.

——, *The Making of Central and Eastern Europe,* The Polish Research Centre, London, 1949.

Esipov, G., *Raskolnichii dela XVIII v.*, St. Petersburg, 1861–1863, 2 vols. Sources.

Evans, S., *The Churches in the U. S. S. R.*, Pilot Press, London, 1943.

Fedotov, G., *The Russian Church Since the Revolution*, S. P. C. K., London, 1928.

——, *Sviatye Drevnei Rusi*, Y.M.C.A. Press, Paris, 1931.

——, *The Russian Religious Mind*, Harvard University Press, 1946. Good.

Filippov, *Istoriia Vygovskoi Staroobriadcheskoi pustyni*, Moscow, 1862. Sources.

Florovsky, G., *Puti russkago Bogosloviia*, Y.M.C.A. Press, Paris, 1937. Good.

Georgievsky, Mitropolit Evlogii, *Put' moei zhizni*, Y.M.C.A. Press, Paris, 1947. Informative.

Goetz, L., *Das Kiever Höhlenkloster als Kulturzentrum der vormongolischen Zeit*, M. Waldbauer, Passau, 1904.

Golubinsky, E., *Istoriia Russkoi Tserkvi*, Moscow University Press, 1900–1901, 1 vol. A very extensive bibliography.

Gordillo, M., *Russie, Pensée Religieuse II, depuis l'établissement du Saint Synod, Dictionnaire de Théologie Catholique*, Vols. CXXV–CXXVII, Vacant et Mangenot, edit., Letousey et Ané, Paris, 1938. Fine bibliography.

Grass, K., *Die russischen Sekten*, Hinrich, Leipzig, 1907–1914, 2 vols.

Grekov, B. D., *Kievskaia Rus*, State Press, Moscow, 1944.

Gumilevsky, Archbishop Philaret, *Obzor russkoi Dukhovnoi literatury*, Kharkov University Press, Kharkov, 1859, 2 vols.

Hecker, J., *Religion and Communism*, Chapman & Hall, London, 1933.

Imperial Archeographic Commission in St. Petersburg published since 1841 a great many sources in dozens of volumes, particularly, *Akty Istoricheskie*, 5 vols., *Dopolneniia*, 12 vols., *Akty, Sobrannye Arkheologicheskoi Komissiei*, 3 vols.

Iswolsky, H., *The Light Before Dusk*, Longmans, Green & Co., Inc., London, 1941.

——, *Soul of Russia*, Sheed & Ward, Inc., London, 1944.

Ivanovsky, N., *Rukovodstvo po istorii i oblicheniiu russkago raskola*, Kazan University Press, 1887.

Joseph of Volokolamsk, *Prosvetitel*, Kazan, 1857. Sources.

Kapterev, N., *Patriarkh Nikon i Tsar Aleksei Mikhailovich,* Holy Trinity Lavra Press, Sergiev Posad, 1909–1912, 2 vols.

Kliuchevsky, V., *A History of Russia,* Dent, London, 1911–1913, 5 vols.

Koialovich, M., *Litovskaia Tserkovnaia Uniia,* St. Petersburg, 1859.

Kudinov, N., *Stoletie Molokanstva v Rossii (1805–1905),* Baku, 1909.

Kutepov, C., *Sekty Khlystov i Skoptsov,* T. Timofeev's Printing Press, Stavropol, 1900.

Lebedev, V., *Istoriia S.S.S.R. do XIX-go veka,* Moscow University Press, 1945.

Ledit, J., *Russie, Pensée Religieuse I, jusqu'à l'établissement du Saint Synode, Dictionnaire de Théologie Catholique,* Vols. CXXIV–CXXV, Paris, 1938. Fine bibliography.

Leib, B., *Rome, Kiev et Byzance à la fin du XI siècle (1088–1099),* Picard, Paris, 1924.

Leroy-Beaulieu, A., *The Empire of the Tsars and the Russians,* Putnam, New York, 1893–1896, 3 vols.

Lileev, J. M., *Iz istorii raskola na Vetke i Starodubie XVII–XVIII v.,* Korchak-Novitsky's Printing Press, Kiev, 1895.

Miliukov, P., *Outlines of Russian Culture,* University of Pennsylvania Press, Philadelphia, 1942, 3 vols.; 1948, 1-vol. edition.

Mirsky, D., *A History of Russian Literature,* Alfred A. Knopf, New York, 1927.

Mochulsky, C., *V. Soloviev,* Y.M.C.A. Press, Paris, 1937. Extremely good.

Moroshkin, M., *Iezuity v Rossii s tsarstvovaniia Ekateriny II do nyneshnikh vremen,* Imperial Chancery, St. Petersburg, 1870.

Nikolsky, N., *Istoriia Russkoi Tserkvi,* Atheist, Moscow, 1930. Curious information.

Nil Sorsky, *Tvoreniia,* St. Petersburg, 1864. Sources.

Oljanchyn, D., *Hryhorij Skoworoda,* Berlin, 1929.

Palmer, W., *The Patriarch Nikon,* Trübner, London, 1871–1876, 6 vols.

Pascal, P., *Avvakum et les débuts du Raskol,* Istina, Paris, 1938. Has a very extensive bibliography.

Pierling, P., *La Russie et le Saint Siège,* Plon-Nourrit, Paris, 1896–1901, 3 vols.

Polnoe Sobranie Zakonov Rossiiskoi Imperii, 3 collections, 82 vols., St. Petersburg, 1830–1916. Sources.

Pravoslavnaia Bogoslovskaia Entsiklopediia, Edit. Prof. Lopukhin, St. Petersburg, 1900–1907, 8 vols.

Priselkov, M., *Ocherki po tserkovno-politicheskoi istorii Kievskoi Rusi,* St. Petersburg, 1913.

Prugavin, A., *Staroobriadchestvo vo vtoroi polovine XIX-go veka,* Sytin, Moscow, 1904.

Raevsky, S., *Ukrainskaia Avtokefalnaia Tserkov,* Jordanville, New York, 1948.

Reutsky, N., *Liudi Bozhii i Skoptsy,* Grachev Printers, Moscow, 1872.

Rouet de Journel, M. J., *Un Collège de Jesuites à St. Petersbourg,* Perrin, Paris, 1922.

——, *Madame Swetchine,* Bonne Presse, Paris, 1929.

Rushbrooke, J. H., *The Baptist Movement on the Continent of Europe,* Carey Press, London, 1923.

——, *Some Chapters of European Baptist History,* Kingsgate Press, London, 1929.

——, *Baptists in the U.S.S.R.,* Kingsgate Press, London, 1943.

Russkaia Istoricheskaia Biblioteka, Arkheologicheskaia Komissiia, St. Petersburg, 1872–1926, 34 vols.

Russkii Biograficheskii Slovar', Imperial Historical Society, St. Petersburg, 1896–1918, 25 vols.

Russkii Entsiklopedicheskii Slovar', Brokhaus and Efron, St. Petersburg, 1890–1904, 41 vols.

Russkiia Letopisi, Polnoe Sobranie, Arkheologicheskaia Komissiia, St. Petersburg, 1872–1918, 24 vols. Sources.

Ryabushinsky, V., *Staroobriadchestvo i russkoe religioznoe chuvstvo,* Private Edition, Joinville-le-Pont, 1936. Valuable.

Sbornik Pravitelstvennykh Svedenii o raskole, Edit. Kelsiev, London, 1860–1862, 4 vols. Very rare.

Sbornik Russkago istoricheskago obstchestva, St. Petersburg, 1867–1916, 148 vols.

Schmurlo, *Russkie Katoliki kontsa XVII-go veka,* Belgrade, 1931.

Shilder, N., *Imperator Aleksandr I,* Suvorin, St. Petersburg, 1904, 4 vols.

——, *Imperator Nikolai I,* Suvorin, St. Petersburg, 1908, 2 vols.

Smirnov, P. S., *Sporui i razdeleniia v russkom raskole v pervoi chetverti XVIII veka,* M. Merkushev's Printing Press, St. Petersburg, 1909. Good.

Strakhovsky, L., *L'Empereur Nicholas Ier et l'esprit national russe,* Librairie Universitaire, Louvain, 1928.

Subbotin, N. I., *Materialy dlia istorii raskola,* Bratstvo Sv. Petra Mitropolita, Moscow, 1875–1895, 9 vols.

———, *Istoriia tak nasyvaemago Avstriiskago ili Belokrinitskago sviashchenstva*, Lissner Printing Press, Moscow, 1895–1899, 2 vols.
Sumner, B. H., *Survey of Russian History*, Reynal & Hitchcock, New York, 1943.

Timasheff, N., *Religion in Soviet Russia*, Sheed & Ward, Inc., New York, 1942.
Tolstoy, D., *Le Catholicisme Romain en Russie*, Dentu, Paris, 1863–1864, 2 vols.
Tolstoy, N., *Russkiia Sviatyni i Drevnosti*, Moscow, 1861–1866, 3 vols.

Vernadsky, G., *Political and Diplomatic History of Russia*, Little, Brown & Company, Boston, 1936.
———, *Ancient Russia*, Yale University Press, 1943.

Wright, J. F. C., *Slava Bohu, The Story of the Dukhobors*, Farrar & Rinehart, Inc., New York, 1940.

Yaroslavsky, E., *Religion in the U.S.S.R.*, International Publishers, New York, 1934.
Yasevich-Borodaevskaia, V., *Borba za veru*, State Printing Press, St. Petersburg, 1912.

Zernov, N., *Moscow the Third Rome*, S.P.C.K., London, 1937.
———, *St. Sergius, Builder of Russia*, S.P.C.K., London, 1937.
———, *The Russians and Their Church*, S.P.C.K., London, 1945.
Zhmakin, V., *Mitropolit Daniil i ego sochineniia*, Imperatorskoe Obstchestvo Istorii i Drevnostei Rossiiskikh, Moscow, 1881.